THE
TETON SIOUX

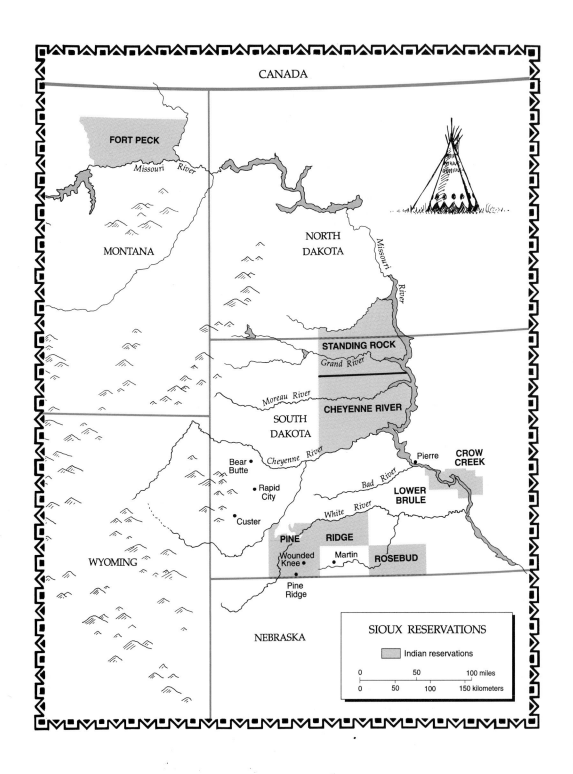

CANADA

FORT PECK

Missouri River

MONTANA

NORTH DAKOTA

Missouri River

STANDING ROCK

Grand River

Moreau River

CHEYENNE RIVER

SOUTH DAKOTA

Bear Butte •

Cheyenne River

• Rapid City

Pierre •

CROW CREEK

Bad River

LOWER BRULE

• Custer

White River

PINE   RIDGE

Wounded Knee •   • Martin   ROSEBUD

Pine Ridge •

WYOMING

NEBRASKA

SIOUX RESERVATIONS

Indian reservations

0   50   100 miles
0   50   100   150 kilometers

THE
TETON
SIOUX

Nancy Bonvillain
New School for Social Research

Frank W. Porter III
General Editor

CHELSEA HOUSE PUBLISHERS
New York   Philadelphia

On the cover A decorative blanket medallion belonging to Red Cloud, a distinguished Teton leader who worked for peace and justice for his people in the late 1800s.

Chelsea House Publishers

Editorial Director Richard Rennert
Executive Managing Editor Karyn Gullen Browne
Copy Chief Robin James
Picture Editor Adrian G. Allen
Art Director Robert Mitchell
Manufacturing Director Gerald Levine
Production Assistant Lisa Yaccino

Indians of North America
Senior Editor Sean Dolan

Staff for **THE TETON SIOUX**
Editorial Assistant Annie McDonnell
Senior Designer Rae Grant
Assistant Designer John Infantino
Picture Researcher Alan Gottlieb

First Printing

1 3 5 7 9 8 6 4 2

Library of Congress Cataloging-in-Publication Data

Bonvillain, Nancy.
    The Teton Sioux / Nancy Bonvillain; Frank W. Porter III, general editor.
        p.   cm.—(Indians of North America)
    Includes bibliographical references and index.
    ISBN 0-7910-1688-9.
        0-7910-2146-7 (pbk.)
    1. Teton Indians—Juvenile literature. [1. Teton Indians. 2. Indians of North America—Great Plains.] I. Porter, Frank W., 1947–
II. Title. III. Series: Indians of North America (Chelsea House Publishers)
E99.T34B66   1994   93-44436
977'.004975—dc20   CIP
                                                     AC

970.00497

18.95

CONTENTS

INDIANS OF NORTH AMERICA

The Abenaki

The Apache

The Arapaho

The Archaeology
  of North America

The Aztecs

The Blackfoot

The Cahuilla

The Catawbas

The Cherokee

The Cheyenne

The Chickasaw

The Chinook

The Chipewyan

The Choctaw

The Chumash

The Coast Salish Peoples

The Comanche

The Creeks

The Crow

Federal Indian Policy

The Hidatsa

The Hopi

The Huron

The Innu

The Inuit

The Iroquois

The Kiowa

The Kwakiutl

The Lenapes

Literatures of the
  American Indian

The Lumbee

The Maya

The Menominee

The Modoc

The Mohawk

The Nanticoke

The Narragansett

The Navajos

The Nez Perce

The Ojibwa

The Osage

The Paiute

The Pawnee

The Pima-Maricopa

The Potawatomi

The Powhatan Tribes

The Pueblo

The Quapaws

The Sac and Fox

The Santee Sioux

The Seminole

The Shawnee

The Shoshone

The Tarahumara

The Teton Sioux

The Tunica-Biloxi

Urban Indians

The Wampanoag

Women in American
  Indian Society

The Yakima

The Yankton Sioux

The Yuma

The Zuni

CHELSEA HOUSE PUBLISHERS

INDIANS OF NORTH AMERICA: CONFLICT AND SURVIVAL

Frank W. Porter III

The Indians survived our open intention of wiping them out, and since the tide turned they have even weathered our good intentions toward them, which can be much more deadly.

John Steinbeck
America and Americans

When Europeans first reached the North American continent, they found hundreds of tribes occupying a vast and rich country. The newcomers quickly recognized the wealth of natural resources. They were not, however, so quick or willing to recognize the spiritual, cultural, and intellectual riches of the people they called Indians.

The Indians of North America examines the problems that develop when people with different cultures come together. For American Indians, the consequences of their interaction with non-Indian people have been both productive and tragic. The Europeans believed they had "discovered" a "New World," but their religious bigotry, cultural bias, and materialistic world view kept them from appreciating and understanding the people who lived in it. All too often they attempted to change the way of life of the indigenous people. The Spanish conquistadores wanted the Indians as a source of labor. The Christian missionaries, many of whom were English, viewed them as potential converts. French traders and trappers used the Indians as a means to obtain pelts. As Francis Parkman, the 19th-century historian, stated, "Spanish civilization crushed the Indian; English civilization scorned and neglected him; French civilization embraced and cherished him."

7

Nearly 500 years later, many people think of American Indians as curious vestiges of a distant past, waging a futile war to survive in a Space Age society. Even today, our understanding of the history and culture of American Indians is too often derived from unsympathetic, culturally biased, and inaccurate reports. The American Indian, described and portrayed in thousands of movies, television programs, books, articles, and government studies, has either been raised to the status of the "noble savage" or disparaged as the "wild Indian" who resisted the westward expansion of the American frontier.

Where in this popular view are the real Indians, the human beings and communities whose ancestors can be traced back to ice-age hunters? Where are the creative and indomitable people whose sophisticated technologies used the natural resources to ensure their survival, whose military skill might even have prevented European settlement of North America if not for devastating epidemics and disruption of the ecology? Where are the men and women who are today diligently struggling to assert their legal rights and express once again the value of their heritage?

The various Indian tribes of North America, like people everywhere, have a history that includes population expansion, adaptation to a range of regional environments, trade across wide networks, internal strife, and warfare. This was the reality. Europeans justified their conquests, however, by creating a mythical image of the New World and its native people. In this myth, the New World was a virgin land, waiting for the Europeans. The arrival of Christopher Columbus ended a timeless primitiveness for the original inhabitants.

Also part of this myth was the debate over the origins of the American Indians. Fantastic and diverse answers were proposed by the early explorers, missionairies, and settlers. Some thought that the Indians were descended from the Ten Lost Tribes of Israel, others that they were descended from inhabitants of the lost continent of Atlantis. One writer suggested that the Indians had reached North America in another Noah's ark.

A later myth, perpetrated by many historians, focused on the relentless persecution during the past five centuries until only a scattering of these "primitive" people remained to be herded onto reservations. This view fails to chronicle the overt and covert ways in which the Indians successfully coped with the intruders.

All of these myths presented one-sided interpretations that ignored the complexity of European and American events and policies. All left serious questions unanswered. What were the origins of the American Indians? Where did they come from? How and when did they get to the New World? What was their life—their culture—really like?

In the late 1800s, anthropologists and archaeologists in the Smithsonian Institution's newly created Bureau of American Ethnology in Washington,

D.C., began to study scientifically the history and culture of the Indians of North America. They were motivated by an honest belief that the Indians were on the verge of extinction and that along with them would vanish their languages, religious beliefs, technology, myths, and legends. These men and women went out to visit, study, and record data from as many Indian communities as possible before this information was forever lost.

By this time there was a new myth in the national consciousness. American Indians existed as figures in the American past. They had performed a historical mission. They had challenged white settlers who trekked across the continent. Once conquered, however, they were supposed to accept graciously the way of life of their conquerors.

The reality again was different. American Indians resisted both actively and passively. They refused to lose their unique identity, to be assimilated into white society. Many whites viewed the Indians not only as members of a conquered nation but also as "inferior" and "unequal." The rights of the Indians could be expanded, contracted, or modified as the conquerors saw fit. In every generation, white society asked itself what to do with the American Indians. Their answers have resulted in the twists and turns of federal Indian policy.

There were two general approaches. One way was to raise the Indians to a "higher level" by "civilizing" them. Zealous missionaries considered it their Christian duty to elevate the Indian through conversion and scanty education. The other approach was to ignore the Indians until they disappeared under pressure from the ever-expanding white society. The myth of the "vanishing Indian" gave stronger support to the latter option, helping to justify the taking of the Indians' land.

Prior to the end of the 18th century, there was no national policy on Indians simply because the American nation had not yet come into existence. American Indians similarly did not possess a political or social unity with which to confront the various Europeans. They were not homogeneous. Rather, they were loosely formed bands and tribes, speaking nearly 300 languages and thousands of dialects. The collective identity felt by Indians today is a result of their common experiences of defeat and/or mistreatment at the hands of whites.

During the colonial period, the British crown did not have a coordinated policy toward the Indians of North America. Specific tribes (most notably the Iroquois and the Cherokee) became military and political pawns used by both the crown and the individual colonies. The success of the American Revolution brought no immediate change. When the United States acquired new territory from France and Mexico in the early 19th century, the federal government wanted to open this land to settlement by homesteaders. But the Indian tribes that lived on this land had signed treaties with European governments assuring their title to the land. Now the United States assumed legal responsibility for honoring these treaties.

At first, President Thomas Jefferson believed that the Louisiana Purchase contained sufficient land for both the Indians and the white population. Within a generation, though, it became clear that the Indians would not be allowed to remain. In the 1830s the federal government began to coerce the eastern tribes to sign treaties agreeing to relinquish their ancestral land and move west of the Mississippi River. Whenever these negotiations failed, President Andrew Jackson used the military to remove the Indians. The southeastern tribes, promised food and transportation during their removal to the West, were instead forced to walk the "Trail of Tears." More than 4,000 men, woman, and children died during this forced march. The "removal policy" was successful in opening the land to homesteaders, but it created enormous hardships for the Indians.

By 1871 most of the tribes in the United States had signed treaties ceding most or all of their ancestral land in exchange for reservations and welfare. The treaty terms were intended to bind both parties for all time. But in the General Allotment Act of 1887, the federal government changed its policy again. Now the goal was to make tribal members into individual landowners and farmers, encouraging their absorption into white society. This policy was advantageous to whites who were eager to acquire Indian land, but it proved disastrous for the Indians. One hundred thirty-eight million acres of reservation land were subdivided into tracts of 160, 80, or as little as 40 acres, and allotted tribe members on an individual basis. Land owned in this way was said to have "trust status" and could not be sold. But the surplus land—all Indian land not allotted to individuals—was opened (for sale) to white settlers. Ultimately, more than 90 million acres of land were taken from the Indians by legal and illegal means.

The resulting loss of land was a catastrophe for the Indians. It was necessary to make it illegal for Indians to sell their land to non-Indians. The Indian Reorganization Act of 1934 officially ended the allotment period. Tribes that voted to accept the provisions of this act were reorganized, and an effort was made to purchase land within preexisting reservations to restore an adequate land base.

Ten years later, in 1944, federal Indian policy again shifted. Now the federal government wanted to get out of the "Indian business." In 1953 an act of Congress named specific tribes whose trust status was to be ended "at the earliest possible time." This new law enabled the United States to end unilaterally, whether the Indians wished it or not, the special status that protected the land in Indian tribal reservations. In the 1950s federal Indian policy was to transfer federal responsibility and jurisdiction to state governments, encourage the physical relocation of Indian peoples from reservations to urban areas, and hasten the termination, or extinction, of tribes.

Between 1954 and 1962 Congress passed specific laws authorizing the termination of more than 100 tribal groups. The stated purpose of the termination policy was to ensure the full and complete integration of Indians into American society. However, there is a less benign way to interpret this legislation. Even as termination was being discussed in Congress, 133 separate bills were introduced to permit the transfer of trust land ownership from Indians to non-Indians.

With the Johnson administration in the 1960s the federal government began to reject termination. In the 1970s yet another Indian policy emerged. Known as "self-determination," it favored keeping the protective role of the federal government while increasing tribal participation in, and control of, important areas of local government. In 1983 President Reagan, in a policy statement on Indian affairs, restated the unique "government is government" relationship of the United States with the Indians. However, federal programs since then have moved toward transferring Indian affairs to individual states, which have long desired to gain control of Indian land and resources.

As long as American Indians retain power, land, and resources that are coveted by the states and the federal government, there will continue to be a "clash of cultures," and the issues will be contested in the courts, Congress, the White House, and even in the international human rights community. To give all Americans a greater comprehension of the issues and conflicts involving American Indians today is a major goal of this series. These issues are not easily understood, nor can these conflicts be readily resolved. The study of North American Indian history and culture is a necessary and important step toward that comprehension. All Americans must learn the history of the relations between the Indians and the federal government, recognize the unique legal status of the Indians, and understand the heritage and cultures of the Indians of North America.

Black Rock, a Teton Sioux chief, as painted in 1832 by George Catlin, who spent eight years among the Indian peoples of the American West.

THE
SETTING

The Teton (TEE-ton) once inhabited a vast territory in the northern prairies and plains of North America in the present-day states of Minnesota, North and South Dakota, Nebraska, and Wyoming. Today, most Teton people live in or near reservation communities within the region of their traditional lands.

The Teton are one of seven divisions or "bands" of American Indians known collectively as the Sioux or the Lakota. The name *Sioux* comes from the language of the nearby Chippewa tribe, who used their word *Nadoweisiweg*, which means "Lesser Snakes," to label their neighbors. When, in the 17th century, French traders heard the Chippewa word, they shortened it to *Sioux*. The people call themselves *Lakota*, meaning "allies" or "friends." In some dialects, the word is pronounced with a *d* as Dakota, from which the states of North and South Dakota get their name.

The Teton band is the westernmost Lakota division. The name *Teton* comes from the native word *tetonwan*, meaning "dwellers of the prairie." The six other Lakota bands can be grouped into a northern and an eastern section. The northern peoples are called the Yankton, from the native word *ihanktunwan*, meaning "dwellers of the end." This group consists of the Yankton and the Yanktonai, or the "little Yankton." The eastern peoples are called the Santee Lakota, a term derived from the word *isanti*, meaning "knife." The name comes from their location near Knife Lake in present-day Minnesota. The Santee consist of four bands, named the Wahpeton ("dwellers among the leaves"), Mdewakanton ("people of Spirit Lake"), Wahpekute ("shooters among the leaves"), and the Sisseton ("camping among the swamps").

The seven Lakota divisions refer to themselves collectively as members of the Seven Council Fires. They are distinct social and political entities, but they recognize a common culture and heritage. They speak separate dialects of the Lakota language and share most characteristics of history, economy, social systems, and religious beliefs. Members of the Seven Council Fires were never integrated into a fixed political structure or confederacy, but they all agreed never to fight one another. They often had common interests and helped each other in times of need.

Of all the Lakota divisions, the Teton are the most numerous. The Teton themselves are composed of a number of distinct bands. The largest group is the Oglala, a name meaning "they scatter their own." Next in size are the Sicangu or "burnt thighs." These people are sometimes referred to today as the Brulé, from the French word meaning "burnt." The other five Teton bands are called the Hunkpapa ("those who camp at the entrance"), Sihasapa ("blackfeet"), Itazipco ("without bows"), Oohenonpa ("two kettles"), and Miniconjou ("those who plant by the stream").

Of all these separate names, only the derivation of the Sicangu or "burnt thighs" has been convincingly documented. According to the people themselves, an event that occurred in the winter of 1762–63 gave them their name. In the words of historian George Hyde:

> The band was encamped on the shore of a long, narrow lake in eastern South Dakota. The grass of the prairie caught fire. A man, his wife, and some children, who were out on the prairie, were burned to death; the rest of the Sioux saved themselves by leaping into the lake; but most of

the Indians had their legs and thighs badly burnt, and scars resulted. The band was therefore given the new name of "Sichangu" or "Burnt Thighs."

The name "tetonwan" (dwellers of the prairie) well describes the original territory of this people. They inhabited the prairies of North America for hundreds of years, living in what is now central Minnesota. They built their villages along the eastern banks of the Missouri River and in the upper valleys of the Minnesota River. In the rich fields, Teton women planted gardens of corn, beans, and squash. They supplemented these foods by gathering wild rice, roots, tubers, and fruits. Teton men hunted animals roaming the prairies and forests nearby. They especially prized the buffalo, which migrated across the prairies in huge herds, but they also hunted deer and elk in the woods.

In addition to procuring their own resources by farming, hunting, and gathering wild plants, the Teton traded with neighboring peoples for other goods. Nearby lived native peoples known as the Arikara and the Mandan, who planted larger fields than did the Teton and usually produced a surplus of food. The Teton often traded with them, obtaining farm crops. In return, the Teton gave their neighbors animal meat and the hides of buffalo, deer, and elk.

By the 17th century, the Lakota, Arikara, and Mandan had very distinct cultures, but at some time in the past their ways of life may have been more similar. Evidence of the common ancestry of

A Santee Lakota encampment in Minnesota, as portrayed by Seth Eastman for the 19th-century explorer Henry Rowe Schoolcraft's study of Native American peoples.

Catlin's view of the Mandan villages on the Missouri River, some 1800 miles above St. Louis. The Mandan were trading partners of the Lakota.

these peoples comes from the study of their languages. Each group now speaks its own separate language, but they all belong to a family of related languages that modern linguists call the Siouan family. Siouan languages share many characteristics of sounds, grammar, and vocabulary. The current languages may be descendants of a common language spoken thousands of years ago by ancestors of modern Siouan peoples.

The Teton continued to live on the prairies of Minnesota until the middle of the 18th century. By that time, far-reaching changes had occurred in North America—changes that came to have a critical influence on the lives not only of the Lakota but of all American Indian peoples of the continent.

Fundamental changes in Native American societies were set in motion by the arrival of Europeans on the shores of North America. At first, Europeans were few in number and of little consequence, but their impact on indigenous peoples grew steadily. By the middle of the 17th century, many changes in native life were already taking place. Of utmost importance was the dislocation of American Indians from their ancestral territories as the result of the presence of Europeans. This process began among peoples who originally lived near the Atlantic coast and in nearby inland areas. Many people were killed in attacks by Europeans who wanted to take land for their own settlements. Others were killed in intertribal wars resulting from competition among American Indians for the remaining land and resources.

Still others, probably the greatest number, died from many devastating diseases that swept through native villages after the Europeans' arrival. These deaths were caused mostly by epidemics of smallpox and measles. Before contact with Europeans, microorganisms that cause smallpox and measles were unknown in North America. Since the germs did not exist in American Indian communities, the people had never developed resistances or immunities to them. When Europeans arrived, carrying with them these deadly organisms, Native Americans had no natural protection. As a consequence, disease spread with sudden and horrifying swiftness. In many instances, whole families and even entire villages became sick and died. Even those people who survived were often left weak and frightened.

As a result of the combination of European expansion, increased warfare, and disease, American Indians in eastern North America saw their lands diminished in size and their lives changed forever. Some continued to reside in a small portion of their ancestral homelands. But many others decided to leave the area, hoping to find peace and prosperity farther west. However, western lands were occupied by other native peoples, so a steady process of westward movement and relocation of numerous groups continued for many years.

A 19th-century photograph of the Black Hills, which the Lakota consider sacred and whites covet for their rich mineral resources.

These events provide the setting in which the Teton found themselves by the 18th century. As the pressures resulting from the dislocation of eastern peoples increased, the Lakota decided to leave their villages on the prairies. They were reacting to the presence of new American Indian groups who entered the prairies, and of French and British traders and soldiers who made their way into the area.

The Teton were the first of the Lakota to cross the Missouri River, heading west onto the Great Plains sometime around 1750. They migrated into present-day South Dakota, reaching the Black Hills by 1765. The Teton continued to interact with other bands of Lakota, who soon followed them onto the plains. They also continued to trade with the Arikara and Mandan, making periodic trading expeditions to these people, who remained in their villages east of the Missouri River.

Once on the plains, the Teton came into contact with other peoples who resided in the area, including the Chey-enne, Pawnee, Arapaho, and Crow. Some, like the Pawnee, were farmers living in settled villages. Others, such as the Cheyenne and Crow, were nomadic and obtained their food from hunting and gathering wild plants.

On the plains, the Teton gave up their farming economy and their settled village life. Instead they became nomadic, establishing temporary camps and small villages. Over the course of the next 100 years, the Teton developed a distinct and thriving culture that grew out of their new circumstances. They adapted to their environment and to an altered way of life. Although this new way required different skills, the Teton met the challenge of change and prospered during this critical period. ▲

By the 19th century, horses had become an integral part of the culture of the Plains Indians, including the Teton Lakota.

TETON
WAYS
OF
LIVING

Teton culture of the 18th century combined traditional practices and new ways of living. After the Teton migrated into the Great Plains, they adapted their traditional knowledge and skills to suit their new surroundings. They also adopted new elements as the need and opportunity arose.

Perhaps the most important innovation in Teton culture was the incorporation of horses into their economy. Ancient species of horses had existed in North America many thousands of years ago, but they became extinct long before the ancestors of American Indians arrived on the continent. Thousands of years later, modern horses were brought to North America by Europeans. The Teton, like other American Indians living on the open plains, immediately realized the enormous potential for travel and transport afforded by use of horses. They therefore began to trade for them in large numbers.

When the Teton crossed the Missouri River around 1750, horses were just beginning to make their appearance in the northern plains. Most of these animals were obtained through trading networks originating in the South and the Southwest. Native groups such as the Comanche and Kiowa got horses by trading with or raiding Spanish settlements in present-day Texas and New Mexico. Other American Indians traded with the Comanche to obtain horses. Several groups, such as the Cheyenne, became middlemen to more northerly peoples, including the Teton. Although the Teton valued horses highly, they did not acquire as many as some Plains groups, as the climate in the region limited the number of horses that the Teton could maintain. Since Teton territory was located in the northern plains, winters were extremely cold and it was difficult to find enough grass for horses to eat during the long winter months.

Catlin's portrayal of a Teton Lakota buffalo hunt. The buffalo provided the Sioux with food, shelter, and clothing, and the animal occupied a central place in the Sioux religion.

In a short period of time, the use of horses revolutionized the economies of all Plains peoples, including the Teton. The Teton emphasized hunting buffalo as their primary means of subsistence. Travel by horseback allowed hunters to go farther from their camps in order to locate the migrating herds. By using horses to carry meat and hides back to camp, men could make more efficient use of their time and effort by killing more buffalo during a single hunting expedition. In centuries prior to acquiring horses, the Teton had used dogs to carry loads, but horses could obviously carry and pull much heavier burdens. As an indication of the importance which the Teton gave to horses, they called these animals *sunka wakan,* an expression meaning "sacred dog."

Teton men used a number of methods for hunting buffalo. In some cases, individual hunters tracked and attacked single animals. Their hunting gear consisted of wooden lances, or bows and arrows tipped with stone arrowheads. In other cases, hunting parties made up of several men traveled and worked together, attacking larger numbers of animals. And in the massive communal buffalo hunts which occurred every summer, hundreds of Teton men united to kill huge numbers of animals.

Several strategies were used in hunting. One tactic involved surrounding a group of buffalo with a circle of small fires lit on the plains grass. The animals were confined within the circle since they were afraid of crossing over fire. They were then easily killed by the hunters.

Teton hunters also commonly used a method of stampeding buffalo over the edge of a cliff. In this method, all able-bodied residents of a camp contributed their labor. Women, children, and older men positioned themselves in lines forming a V to surround a herd of buffalo. The open end of the V led toward a cliff. Then hunters stampeded the herd

by shouting and making loud noises to frighten the animals. As the buffalo ran, the women and children continued to shout at them from the sidelines to keep the animals within the V formation. The buffalo blindly plunged over the edge of the cliff. Many died in the fall itself. Others were killed by hunters waiting for them below.

The same basic method was used to drive a herd of buffalo into a corral put up on the plains by forming piles of stone and brush to make an enclosure. Animals stampeding into the corral were easily killed by the waiting hunters.

Once the animals were killed, Teton women had much work to do. First they cut the meat into smaller pieces so that it could be carried back to camp. Some meat was cooked immediately and eaten on that day, but most of it was preserved for later use. Women cut the meat into thin strips and hung it on wooden racks to dry. Afterward, they packed the dried meat into tight bundles and stored it in their homes. When needed for food, meat was boiled along with wild berries or plants added for variety and flavor. Some of the dried meat was used to make *pemmican.* Pemmican was prepared by pounding the meat into a powder and mixing it with dried berries. These various methods of preserving meat ensured that supplies obtained in one hunting expedition could sustain the people for a long period of time.

Many other aspects of Teton culture demonstrate the people's ability to adapt to their environment and their circum-

This Lakota woman, according to Catlin, was esteemed as a great beauty. "She was beautifully dressed in skins," he wrote, "ornamented profusely with brass buttons and beads. Her hair was plaited . . . and over her other dress she wore a handsomely garnished buffalo robe."

stances. Their tools, utensils, and housing were all lightweight and easy to transport. Teton men and women used wood and animal bone in crafting some of their equipment, including many types of hammers, knives, awls, clubs, bows, arrows, and lances.

The Teton also made much use of animal hides and wood to construct their living quarters. The Teton resided in structures known as *tipis*. A tipi is a cone-shaped home, rounded at its base and tapered to an open smoke hole at the top. Most tipis were approximately 12 to 16 feet in diameter at the base. They were large enough to house a family of parents and children and perhaps a few additional relatives.

Teton men and women combined their labor in constructing tipis. Women trimmed eight to twelve buffalo skins so that they fit together exactly. Then they sewed the hides together with strong sinew. Meanwhile, men put up a frame made of wooden poles to support the hides. At the top of the tipi, two buffalo skins were loosely hung at the central smoke hole. The flaps could be opened to allow smoke to leave the tipi. They could be closed to keep out rain, snow, or cold air. The bottom of the tipi was held in place on the ground by stones spaced around the edge of the hides. But in hot weather, people rolled the bottom skins up so that fresh air could pass into the tipi. When constructing a tipi, space was left open for a doorway, but it was covered with an extra hide that was held in place with pins made of wood or bone when people wanted it closed.

Tipis had few furnishings. People used buffalo hides for seating, bedding, and covers. A hearth was built in the center of the tipi for cooking and heating.

Some men drew paintings on the skins of their tipis. They used natural dyes to make pictographs that recorded important events. Successful hunting expeditions or bravery in warfare were favorite subjects for the paintings.

Despite their size, tipis were lightweight and could be taken apart in a matter of minutes when people moved to another location. The wooden poles were attached to the back of a horse and the hides were rolled up and placed on the poles.

Many utensils, equipment, and articles of clothing were also made from hides. Some objects were made from buffalo hides, while others were fashioned from the skins of deer or elk. In order to convert hides into useful items, Teton women tanned them to make them soft. In the tanning process, the raw hide was scraped with a blade made of elk antler to remove all animal flesh and fat. If the women planned to make the skins into clothing or tipis, they removed the animal's hair from the hide. Hair was left on hides used for bedding and covers. Once the hide was cleaned, it was soaked in water until it became pliable. In the final step of tanning, oils and fats were carefully rubbed into the hide to keep it soft.

In addition to using animal skins for tipis and furnishings, Teton women made numerous kinds of containers out of buffalo, deer, and elk hides. Pouches of various sizes held food, clothing, ornaments, and other personal objects.

Prior to their migration onto the Great Plains, Teton women had made earthen pottery, but when the people became nomadic hunters and gatherers, they gave up the art because pottery was too often broken in transport. One of the earlier uses of pottery had been in cooking, but later, Teton women invented a new technique for preparing food. They first dug a pit in the ground, lined it with animal skins, and filled it with water. Then they heated stones on a fire until they were red-hot and placed them in the water. Heat from the stones made the water boil so that food could be cooked. Spoons made of buffalo horns were used for stirring and serving food, but they were not used when eating.

Instead, people simply ate with their fingers.

Teton women were responsible for making articles of clothing worn by all the people. Most items were sewn from soft, tanned skins of deer and elk. Women generally wore knee-length dresses and leggings reaching up to the knee. Men wore sleeveless shirts, breechcloths, and leggings which reached well above the knee. In cold or rainy weather, people covered themselves with warm buffalo robes.

Clothing was often decorated, using two different techniques. Men used dyes to paint designs and pictures on their clothing. Women embroidered dresses, shirts, and moccasins with porcupine quills or beadwork. They made geometric designs and brightly colored shapes. A favorite pattern was an embroidered

A pictograph by Amos Bad-Heart-Bull, an Oglala, depicting a traditional tribal council.

background of blue or white with a design of blue or red.

Men and women wore various kinds of ornaments on their bodies and in their hair. They liked wearing necklaces and armbands of bone or beads. Some people painted or tattooed designs on their face or body. All children had their ears pierced when they were five or six years old. A man generally did the piercing by making a small hole with a bone needle. Then a string of colored beads was worn as an ear ornament.

Most Teton women and men wore their hair in two braids, often intertwined with colored cloth or beads. Older women wore their hair loose on their backs. Some young men preferred a distinctive hairstyle called a "roach." A man achieved this effect by shaving the sides of his head and allowing the hair in the center to grow. Young men also wore single eagle feathers in their hair. Such emblems were signs of a man's success in war. Older war leaders sometimes wore large feather bonnets on ceremonial occasions.

Most Teton lived in family units that consisted of a married couple and their children. Sometimes a relative of one of the spouses resided with the group if he or she had no other family. Teton people traced their kinship relationship through both their mother's and father's relatives. This is a system called bilateral descent. It is the same kind of system familiar to many Americans today.

Even though the Teton considered themselves related to people through both men and women, relatives on one's father's side played a more important role in one's life. For example, Teton settlements typically consisted of families related through men. After marriage, men tended to remain in the camps of their fathers. Groups of brothers formed the core of settlements after their father died. Women often moved away from their parents after marriage to take up residence in their husband's camp.

One reason that related men resided in the same camp was that men had to cooperate in several types of activities. Since hunting was often done communally, men depended on each other for aid. Men also went on raids or to war in small groups requiring the cooperation and support of all. The Teton assumed that relatives worked best together and could depend on each other most. Since work groups usually consisted of men, it was best that related men live in the same camp.

Of course, as in all things, this rule was not always followed. A married couple might decide to live with the wife's family for many reasons. Perhaps the husband had many brothers while the wife had none. In such a case, the wife's parents might ask the couple to live with them so that they would not be left alone. Perhaps the husband did not get along well with his own relatives and preferred to move away. People were free to follow their own inclinations and to make decisions that best suited themselves or their families.

Most Teton marriages were arranged by parents for their daughters and sons. The marriage ceremony consisted of an

Lakota men sneak up on a Crow encampment to steal horses. Such raids were a means for young Lakota braves to demonstrate their courage.

exchange of gifts between the families of the bride and groom. They gave presents to each other to signal their friendship and respect.

Some marriages were not arranged by parents but rather started with the elopement of the couple. A man and woman might have decided on their own that they wanted to marry and just began to live together. If a man and woman were attracted to each other, the man might show his intentions by courting the woman. He would sit outside her tipi at night, playing a wooden flute and singing songs of love. If the woman was also so inclined, she might find rea-

sons to walk alone to fetch water or to collect wood so that she might find a moment to speak privately to the man she liked. Although most Teton people had only one spouse, some families consisted of a husband married to two or more wives. In these cases, the wives usually were sisters. Men involved in such marriages were often wealthy and influential. They might own many horses and be successful hunters or warriors.

Ideally, Teton marriages lasted for a lifetime, but divorces often occurred, particularly early in a couple's life together. Divorce simply involved a couple's decision to separate. Sometimes the decision was made jointly, but in other cases, a husband or wife might choose to end the marriage.

The Teton considered their relatives to be the most important people in their social world. A great deal of respect was shown between fathers and sons and mothers and daughters. People also tended to show respect to their older siblings. Relations between sisters and brothers were especially formal. Once they reached their teens, they rarely socialized or joked together. People behaved respectfully toward their grandparents, and grandparents often showered their grandchildren with affection.

Relations between parents-in-law and their children's spouses were very formal. A woman and her son-in-law ideally avoided being in each other's presence and did not speak to each other directly. If they had to be together, they conducted themselves with great decorum. A son-in-law avoided doing or saying anything that might offend his mother-in-law. This type of behavior was a sign of respect and honor.

The lives of the Teton followed a typical cycle from birth through puberty, adulthood, and death. When a pregnant woman knew she was about to give birth, she stayed in her tipi accompanied by older women who served as midwives. Men were not allowed in the tipi during or soon after delivery. Shortly after birth, the baby was given a personal name by an older male or female relative. As a child grew up, he or she

often received additional personal names based on some physical characteristic or personality trait.

When a girl reached puberty, a special ceremony was held for her. During her first menstruation, the girl went to stay for a few days in a hut built for her outside the camp. Older women accompanied her and instructed her about the work and responsibilities of adult Teton women. She was told how to behave with respect toward others.

Two or three weeks later, the girl's father sponsored a public ceremony and feast to mark the occasion of his daughter's passage to womanhood. The ritual was conducted by a man chosen by the girl's parents. As described by J. R. Walker, a physician who lived among the Oglala for many years in the early 20th century, the ritual leader

> painted red the right side of the young woman's forehead and a red stripe at the parting of her hair, and while doing so he said, "You see your oldest sister on the altar. Her forehead is painted red. Red is a sacred color. Your first menstrual flow was red. You have taken of the red water [red chokecherry juice] on this day. This is to show that you are akin to the Buffalo God and are his woman. You are entitled to paint your face in this manner." He then tied the eagle plume at the crown of her head and said, "The spirit of the eagle and the duck are with you. They will give you the influence of the Sun and the South Wind. They will give you many children."

The pubescent girl was given a new set of clothing as a symbol of her adult status and her new role in the community. Relatives and neighbors attended the ceremony to honor the girl and her family.

A boy's passage to manhood was marked when he achieved success in activities typical of Teton men. For instance, when a boy went hunting and killed his first animal, his family gave a public feast in his honor. When he first joined a raiding or war group, his parents held a similar celebration.

Young adults often engaged in a ritual called a Vision Quest. They sought visions of a supernatural spirit who would afterward become a personal guardian for them. Although Vision Quests were especially important for men, many women also sought supernatural guardians. Before setting out on the quest, men and women prepared themselves by fasting for four days. At the end of this period, they went through ritual purification in a sweat bath. The Teton considered sweats to be sacred events. The act of sweating symbolized shedding of physical and psychological impurities. Sweat baths cleansed people's minds and spirits and prepared them to face the world of supernatural beings.

The Vision Quest itself lasted four days. The seeker left camp alone and proceeded to a place to think and pray for aid. During this period, he or she did not eat or sleep. All the seeker's thoughts and actions focused on encountering a spirit. Seekers offered prayers to the spirit world, asking for guidance. One such prayer, recorded by the great Oglala spiritual leader Black Elk (born in 1863), asks for help for himself and his people:

> Grandfather, I am sending a voice!
> To the Heavens of the universe, I am
> sending a voice,
> That my people may live!

If the quest was successful, a spirit spoke to the seeker and gave him or her special songs or instructions to follow when in danger or need. Afterward, whenever the seeker was in peril or suffered misfortune, he or she could use these songs and prayers to call on the spirit's help.

People often found distinctive objects in their Vision Quests which they kept as tokens of their experience. They might find such items as eagle feathers, oddly shaped stones, or animal bones. These tokens took on personal meaning for the seeker. They were put in pouches and kept at home or carried whenever the seeker traveled from camp.

At the end of life, people were expected to face their death with courage. But after someone died, relatives went into a period of deep mourning. The deceased's body was placed in the branches of a tree or on a scaffold erected for the purpose. Personal objects of the deceased were usually put with the body to comfort the soul. Offerings of food were also typically placed there so the deceased's soul had some nourishment as it journeyed away from this world.

Shell Man, an Oglala warrior painted by Catlin in 1832. Whites often misunderstood the position of individuals in Lakota society. Chiefs, for example, might be esteemed for their wisdom or bravery but had no authority to compel individuals to follow their dictates.

Since the Teton lived in relatively small settlements, they did not develop overarching political structures to govern themselves. Instead they relied on public opinion to ensure that all people adhered to rules of proper behavior. If someone committed an offense against others, people in the community showed their disapproval by publicly ridiculing the wrongdoer. They might gossip about him within earshot or tease him whenever they met. People faced with such public criticism usually felt ashamed and made sure to correct their behavior in the future.

If conflicts arose between members of the community, they could seek advice from a council composed of elder men in the settlement. These men heard arguments presented by the parties concerned and sought additional information when needed. Their decisions had influence in the community but they had no formal or absolute authority. They could not enforce their judgments but instead relied on public opinion to support them.

Leadership by individuals was relatively weak among the Teton. Some men were seen as leaders or chiefs, but their position was unstable. A man was respected as a leader based on his success in hunting or warfare. Other desirable traits included intelligence, generosity, even temper, and skill as an orator. Chiefs were admired and respected but they had no authority over others. They could not force anyone to follow their advice or plans. People heard the chief's opinions and then were free to decide for themselves on the proper course of action.

Although most chiefs remained respected members of their community, if they became arrogant or frequently mistaken in their judgments, people simply began to speak ill of them or ignore them. Such men were no longer thought of as leaders. They lost their position in society because of their own behavior.

In addition to the older men who functioned as chiefs, some young men were known as war leaders. These men were active and successful in raiding or warfare. They were leaders of military expeditions, but membership in war groups was completely voluntary. A leader could speak to other men and present them with his plans for action, but no one was in any way compelled to join the group. However, if a war leader was usually successful, other men were eager to do as he advised. Warfare came to play an important role in the lives of Teton men. It was often motivated by a desire to obtain horses in raids against other tribes. And as competition for land and resources increased in the 19th century, warfare was often necessary as a means of defense against Anglo or American Indian intruders.

Warfare in Plains societies had several ritualistic traits as well. Men who wanted to participate had to follow two rules in the days prior to leaving for war. For four days before setting out, they were not allowed to engage in sexual

This pictograph depicts a ceremony of the deer dreamers, one of several secret Teton societies.

activity. In addition, they underwent ritual purification in a sweat bath. This act cleansed their bodies and spirits, giving them strength and courage to face dangers encountered in conflict.

Actions in raids or war were judged according to complex rules of bravery. The Teton, like other Plains peoples, had a system of noting war exploits called "counting coup." In this system, various actions were ranked on the basis of dangers encountered by a warrior. The most prestigious act was to approach an enemy, attack him at close range, and then get away safely. For example, wounding an enemy by clubbing him brought more honor than shooting from a distance because it meant that the warrior exposed himself to direct danger of retaliation or defeat. Success in face-to-face combat was considered honorable. Other daring actions included wresting a weapon from an enemy's hand or stealing a horse from inside an enemy village.

In addition to civil and war leaders, some Teton men and women gained prestige through their membership in various social groups active in Teton communities. These groups were centered on particular activities. Some were military or ritual societies. Each group had its own songs, dances, and distinctive insignia identifying members. People joined these voluntary groups based on their personal interest and/or selection by members of the group. An invitation to join was made to an interested individual. Then the inductee went through a rite of initiation and presented gifts of thanks to other members.

The most prestigious of the Teton social groups was one named Heyoka. Heyoka were men who received their calling through visions from the spirit world. A spirit appeared to a man either in a dream or while awake and told him that he was chosen to become a Heyoka. Once in the group, Heyoka had to do everything in reverse of the normal pattern. They walked backwards, sat backwards while riding horses, and reversed their clothing. Their actions were both serious and comical to onlookers. This dual role was well explained by the Oglala healer Black Elk in his autobiography. Speaking of the effect of Heyoka on other people, Black Elk said:

> The people shall be made to feel jolly and happy, so that it may be easier for the power to come to them. The truth comes into this world with two faces. One is sad and suffering and the other laughs; but it is the same face, laughing or weeping. When people are already in despair, maybe the laughing face is better for them; and when they feel too good and too sure of being safe, maybe the weeping face is better for them to see.

From time to time, Heyoka men sought visionary contact with spirits in order to strengthen their powers and to receive instruction. A vision seeker fasted and purified himself through a sweat bath. Then he prayed for spiritual aid. Dreams often were important vehicles for contact with spirits. The seeker interpreted episodes depicted in his dreams or he asked other men with spiritual knowledge to determine the meaning of his dreams.

Teton men and women who were thought to have great spiritual powers were among the most respected members of their communities. Many people consulted them, asked their advice, and sought their aid in times of sickness and misfortune. Spiritual leaders were also medical healers. They used many different therapeutic techniques to cure illness. They studied medicinal properties of herbs, tree bark, wild fruits, tubers, and other plants. In addition, healers cured with the aid of spirit guardians whose help they sought in diagnosing the cause of a patient's ailment. Ritual cures often included songs, prayers, and dances aimed at obtaining powers of supernatural forces to cure disease. In addition to their curing abilities, women

Blue Medicine was a medicine man of the Teton, entrusted with the spiritual and physical health of his people.

and men with spiritual powers could foretell future events. They were able to call upon their guardian spirits to receive messages from the supernatural realm.

The supernatural realm of the Teton was inhabited by many different kinds of spirits. All spirit beings and entities were considered *wakan,* or "sacred." The most important beings were sun (*wi*), sky (*skan*), and earth (*maka*). The sun and sky were endowed with male characteristics whereas the earth was thought of as female. The earth was often called all-mother and thus was a symbol of generation, birth, and growth.

Next in importance were spirits of winds, the four cardinal directions of North, South, East, and West, the Thunderers, and spirits of Buffalo and Bear.

A special role in Teton religion was given to a deity called White Buffalo Calf Woman. Her origin is said to have been in the past when there was warfare between human beings and buffalo. After many conflicts, the spirit of Buffalo sent White Buffalo Calf Woman to the people to bring them peace and knowledge. She gave people a Sacred Pipe which they could smoke to send their messages to the supernatural world. The pipe thus creates bonds between inhabitants of natural and spiritual realms of existence. In addition to the gift of the pipe, White Buffalo Calf Woman gave the Teton seven rituals which form the basis of their religious practice. Of these, the four most important rites include the sweat bath, which is performed to purify people's bodies and minds; the Vision Quest through which people seek visions and aid from spirits; the Girl's Puberty Ceremony; and the Sun Dance, performed every summer to give thanks for life, health, and good fortune.

The Sun Dance was a central and dramatic Teton ritual. Sun Dances were held every summer in conjunction with annual buffalo hunts and community social activities. At this time, the separate Teton bands joined together in a large encampment consisting of hundreds of people. Each band had its assigned place in a large circular settlement. The circle was left open toward the east. The Lakota considered the east to be the most sacred direction since it was the place of the rising sun. The east

Many Plains Indians celebrated a variation of the Sun Dance at the conclusion of the summer buffalo hunt. Its purpose, according to anthropologist Ruth Underhill, "was to renew communion with the earth, sun, and the spirits, and especially with the winds, so that the tribe might have health and fertility and the buffalo might never fail."

thus symbolized renewal and growth of the earth and all living creatures.

Preparations for a Sun Dance actually began months before the summertime, when a man or woman voluntarily made a vow to sponsor the ritual. An individual might make a vow to sponsor a dance in thanks for recovery from illness or alleviation from some other misfortune. The sponsor first went to a healer and declared his intention. The healer then began to make plans and set a date for the upcoming event.

Four days of preliminary preparation preceded the actual dance. During

these four days, a group of men chose a special tree for the central pole of the Sun Dance Lodge. This tree was then considered sacred. Once chosen, the tree was approached by men on horseback and set upon in a mock attack as though it were a prized buffalo.

The Sun Dance itself consisted of various events which were held over the next four days. It began with a procession of men and women to the Sacred Tree. The tree was cut down by a group of women. Then all proceeded to the Sun Dance area and set about constructing the Sun Dance Lodge and installing the tree as the central pole. The pole was decorated with feathers, insignia, and an effigy of the spirit of Buffalo. An altar was erected in the lodge, also dedicated to the spirit of Buffalo.

The most dramatic episode of a Sun Dance occurred on the last day. It centered on the activities of several men who had pledged to participate as dancers. Candidates were expected to embody the moral values of Lakota society, including bravery, generosity, fortitude, and personal integrity. As a mark of their special status, they were given shirts of tanned hide painted red and sets of armbands and anklets. The men prepared themselves for their ordeal by praying to spirits, asking for strength, courage, and good fortune. On the day of the Sun Dance, the dancers rose early, watched the rising sun, and walked in a slow procession to the Sun Dance Lodge. Some of these men had pledged to show their bravery by piercing the flesh on their back and chest with small skewers attached to sinew cords tied to the Sun Dance pole. They sang, prayed, and danced in a circular movement around the Sun Dance Lodge. After many hours,

dancers broke free of the cords tying them to the Sun Dance pole, in the process wrenching pieces of skin from their bodies. These acts were considered signs of physical and spiritual daring. Men who engaged in such activity were honored by others in their community.

The Sun Dance ritual drew together all members of the Teton community. It unified them with a common goal of celebrating health and success, and it allowed them to express their gratitude to the spirits for the bounty of the universe. The ritual embodied underlying values of Teton society: the desire for harmony, health, and prosperity and the pledge of cooperation and generosity to one's family and community.

With their ability to transform and adapt their cultural practices and beliefs, the Teton were set to play an important role in the history of American Indian life in the Great Plains. They successfully met challenges from the new setting in which they found themselves. And for a time, they successfully met challenges brought by settlers from European and American societies in the 18th and 19th centuries. ▲

Inevitably, the coming of white fur traders, settlers, and then soldiers altered Lakota culture. Fort Laramie was built by the Rocky Mountain Fur Company on the North Platte River in Wyoming in 1834.

MEETING
THE
CHALLENGE
OF
CHANGE

During a period of 100 years beginning in 1750, the Teton thrived in the northern plains region which had become their homeland. They developed a robust economy based on their use of horses to follow herds of buffalo and to transport increasing amounts of food and goods that the people possessed.

The Teton also adapted to new neighbors and to the constant flow of intruders into the region. In addition to the Teton, other American Indians such as the Cheyenne, Arapaho, and Crow were migrating to the plains. The Teton quickly began to interact and trade with these groups. At first, relations among American Indians living in the plains were generally friendly. But conflicts later erupted among various peoples because of changing circumstances brought about by contact with European and American traders. Trade with European and American merchants first increased the fortunes of American Indians in the plains but then proved to be a cause of conflict in the region.

The Teton became familiar with goods of European manufacture through their ongoing trade with American Indians who remained in the eastern prairies. The Mandan and Arikara living along the Missouri River supplied the Teton with products obtained in trade with Europeans and Americans. The Teton especially prized utensils, tools, and weapons made of metal. They traded for knives, nails, needles, kettles, scissors, and arrowheads. Guns and ammunition also became desirable items. In exchange for manufactured goods, the Teton gave buffalo meat and hides to their trading partners.

Throughout the latter half of the 18th century, Teton men and women made yearly trips to present-day Minnesota to trade with the Mandan and Arikara who obtained European goods from French merchants. The French eagerly expanded their trading networks westward from their original bases in eastern Canada. This trade increased after the French were expelled from the east in

The knife at bottom was obtained by the Oglala in trade with whites in the early 19th century. In trade, Native Americans most desired metal goods: copper kettles, knives and tools, and guns.

1763, when they were defeated by the British in the so-called French and Indian War.

The Teton did not deal directly with French merchants because they had already left their lands in the prairies of Minnesota where the French built trading posts. But they were familiar with French products and traders from earlier times. As early as 1682, the Lakota were visited by a French trader named Pierre LeSueur. In 1695, LeSueur persuaded several Lakota leaders to travel to Montreal to meet with traders there. Some trade between the Lakota and the French continued into the early 1700s while the Lakota remained in their eastern prairie territory. Later, however, when the Teton crossed westward into the plains, their dealings with French merchants became indirect. Since the Teton maintained economic and social relations with other American Indian tribes that remained on the prairies, they obtained French goods through these connections.

An additional source of trade became important to the Teton in the early 19th century. American traders based in St. Louis, Missouri, expanded their businesses by traveling north along the Missouri River. They made direct contact with the Teton and exchanged American products for animal hides and meat hunted by Teton men and prepared for market by Teton women. Although buffalo hides were the Teton's major marketable item, they also traded beaver and muskrat to American merchants.

In addition to trading for their own supplies, the Teton became middlemen between American traders and other American Indians living in the northern plains. Their position as go-between meant that Teton traders increased their own wealth and established economic dominance in the region. Indeed, in 1805, the American explorers Meriwether Lewis and William Clark described the Lakota as the dominant economic and political power along the Missouri River.

The Teton traded with merchants from several American companies. Most important was the American Fur Company of St. Louis. The company built a large trading post at the site of present-day Pierre, South Dakota, as well as some smaller stations along the Missouri River. In the 1830s, competitors from the Rocky Mountain Fur Company began to make inroads into Teton territory. In 1834, merchants from the Rocky Mountain company built their own post on the North Platte River in Wyoming. The trading post, later known as Fort Laramie, became a major commercial center for the Teton region. In addition to the Teton, the Cheyenne and Arapaho traveled to trade at Fort Laramie.

Although the Teton and other American Indians greatly desired implements and weapons that they received from Europeans and Americans, trade created unforeseen problems for them. As their familiarity with manufactured goods increased, items that began as novelties and luxuries quickly became necessities in a changing way of life. The people preferred to obtain metal goods rather than to spend many long hours making utensils from stone and wood as they previously had done. Not only did their traditional methods require much time to create objects, but the items also broke or wore out more quickly than did goods made of metal. In order to obtain growing amounts of manufactured goods, Teton hunters had to hunt and kill more and more buffalo to give to European and American traders. This need forced Teton men to spend more of their time and energy pursuing buffalo. And Teton women had to spend more of their time and energy processing buffalo meat into dried pemmican and tanning buffalo hides for the market.

By the middle of the 19th century, increased trade resulted in depletion of resources in the plains. Buffalo herds became smaller owing to the expansion of hunting made necessary by the needs of trade. Although there were still considerable numbers of buffalo, their decline from previous years created conflict among American Indian peoples over the remaining animals. Conflicts erupted from time to time in warfare and raids of each other's camps. In these attacks, raiders often stole horses from other American Indians. If a man were able to take someone else's horses, he increased his own wealth and ability to travel and transport goods and also decreased his enemy's wealth and freedom of movement.

In addition to economic and technological changes in Teton life directly resulting from trade with Europeans and Americans, some indirect cultural changes also took place. One change involved the way that people regarded themselves and others. Teton society had previously recognized each individual as equal to others. Differences in wealth and status did not exist. In fact, if some people had greater success in hunting than their relatives and neighbors, they customarily shared whatever they had with those in their community who were less skilled or less fortunate. Sharing and generosity were considered extremely important. These norms guaranteed the survival and well-being of all. However, as people amassed horses and goods in large numbers, they began to think of themselves as different based on the amount of possessions that they had. Wealth and rank were measured in many ways, especially in numbers of horses that an individual owned. Horses were a sign of wealth and a sign of daring since a man often obtained many of his horses by raiding other peoples.

Another important effect of trade in Teton life was a change in relations between women and men. In traditional times, husbands and wives were generally close in age and status. Although husbands were usually older than their wives, the difference was of only a few years. People typically married when women were in their later teenage years and men in their late teens or early twenties. Then, during the first half of the 19th century, Teton norms for marriage changed. People preferred that their daughters marry men who had established their reputations as good hunters and warriors. And in order for a man to acquire these skills and reputation, he had to delay marriage, often until he was in his thirties.

At the same time, the age when women married was decreasing. Parents often arranged marriages for daughters when the girls were in their early teens. A reason for this change was connected to another change in marriage customs. In traditional Teton culture, most people were married to one mate. But by the 19th century, some men married more than one woman. Successful and wealthy men sometimes married three or four women and thus established large families for themselves. The reason that men wanted several wives was that as a man hunted and killed many buffalo at a time, he needed the help of more women to prepare dried buffalo meat and to tan buffalo hides for trade. A man with more than one wife was in a better position to increase his wealth through trade than was a man with only one wife. And having several wives also meant that a man would have many children. His sons could help him hunt for more buffalo and his daughters could help their mothers prepare buffalo meat and hides.

This Amos Bad-Heart-Bull pictograph shows three Teton men courting a girl. The ornate robes of the men show that they had established themselves as hunters or warriors.

Teton girls were trained from an early age in the skills of tanning and sewing. They were sought for marriage at a young age by men desiring to expand their wealth. Girls were valued in part because of their ability to process buffalo for the market. And a girl was also valued by her father because when she married, her husband customarily gave gifts of horses to the father. Fathers were thus often persuaded to allow their daughters to marry at early ages to men well into their thirties or beyond.

Finally, as women became increasingly younger than their husbands, their status within their households declined. Age was an important factor in any individual's status. Young people of either gender were expected to be polite and deferential to their elders. Young wives therefore were taught to defer to their husbands.

A further cultural change occurring in the 19th century was an increase in the importance of chiefs. The Teton recognized two different kinds of chiefs: peace chiefs and war chiefs. Peace chiefs were usually elder men who had proven their abilities as successful hunters in their prime. In addition, they often had religious powers and had visionary contacts with guardian spirits. Many chiefs were also healers and could help people recover from serious illness.

Little Bear was a Teton war chief. Traditionally, such leaders were responsible for planning and implementing military maneuvers, but the decision to go to war was not theirs to make.

Peace chiefs were successful in life's experiences and were also men of even temper, great intelligence, and compassion for others. They were generous and shared their wealth with people in need.

War chiefs were usually young men in the prime of life. They were brave and daring in warfare. They continually proved their ability to lead others in successful raids. Although war chiefs had responsibilities to plan and carry out attacks against their enemies, they were under the general authority of elder peace chiefs. Since war chiefs were relatively young, they listened to advice from the elder men. In later Teton history, however, young men sometimes were impatient to attack their enemies. Then they acted without the approval of peace chiefs. This change proved to be a disruptive force in Teton community life in the latter half of the 19th century.

Disruption of Teton life came from other sources as well. Intrusions into Teton territory by American traders, travelers, and settlers increased throughout the 19th century. Populations in eastern states were growing and many eastern farmers heard that there was a large amount of land in the prairies and plains that would be good for cultivation. Many families set out to make new lives for themselves. But the land that they came upon was not unused territory. American Indian villages were not located close together— open lands were important to native peoples. The people used the land for hunting. Each group traditionally con-

trolled a large territory in order to support its community throughout the year.

American settlers and the American government did not respect the American Indians' rights to all of their traditional territory. Farmers and ranchers encroached on American Indians' land. In response, Native American peoples tried to defend their territory, resorting to attacks against intruders after negotiations failed to dissuade the settlers. The United States government and its army rarely sided with the original inhabitants but instead protected settlers. The army attacked the Teton and other American Indians who tried to dislodge the American intruders.

The discovery of gold in California in 1849 created another vast number of American travelers through the plains. Most of these people were merely temporary nuisances, but others decided to stay and set up their farms in the region. Increased encroachments led to intensification of hostilities between American Indians and intruders. This in turn led to expansion of conflict between American Indians and the United States Army. In numerous raids, the army destroyed many American Indian settlements and killed thousands of native people.

Thousands more died from infectious diseases that spread throughout the plains in the 19th century. Epidemics of measles and smallpox spread rapidly in native communities. In a devastating epidemic of smallpox which occurred throughout the plains in 1837, half of the native population perished. Smallpox,

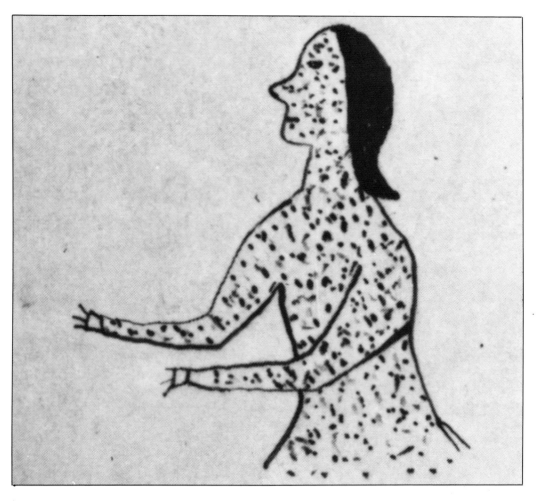

This drawing is one of many made by an Oglala named Short Man to illustrate the history of his people in the 19th century. It was intended to depict the measles epidemic that devastated his people in that year. With no natural immunities, Native American peoples suffered greatly from diseases introduced to North America by Europeans.

measles, and influenza, all diseases of European origin, wrought death in large numbers among American Indian peoples who had never experienced these illnesses and who therefore had no natural immunities or resistances to them. Even survivors were left in a weakened and debilitated condition. They were less able to carry out their normal economic duties or to defend themselves against their enemies.

Another source of foreign intrusion came to the plains in the form of missionary activity. European and American ministers entered the region in the 19th century in order to convert American Indians to Christianity. Missionary activity in the area had actually begun two centuries earlier, when a French Jesuit named Father Jacques Marquette first contacted the Lakota in 1674. Marquette's efforts, however, proved fruitless. Other French missionaries again attempted to convert the Lakota in the 18th century, working among them from 1727 to 1737. These efforts also proved fruitless. But when British and American ministers came to the Lakota in the 19th century, they were more successful in achieving some conversions.

Protestant missionaries working for the United Foreign Mission Society established missions among the Lakota in the 1820s. Presbyterian ministers likewise contacted the Lakota beginning in 1834. They were followed in the 1850s and 1860s by Roman Catholic missionaries. Although the great majority of Teton were not swayed by any of these attempts, Christian workers continued their efforts.

In the 19th century, the United States government decided to proceed with a policy of negotiating treaties with American Indians living in the plains. The government wanted to establish secure zones for American settlement. In order to accomplish this goal, they had to force the original inhabitants to give up some of their land. Some American Indian peoples, including the Teton, were compelled to surrender their land because they felt they were in a desperate situation. The Teton hoped that by agreeing

to terms, the American government would protect the land remaining under Teton control. They hoped that American settlers would not be permitted to encroach on more Teton land.

The history of treaties between the Lakota and the United States government began in the early 19th century with the signing of treaties of "friendship" between the two groups. The first such document was signed in 1816. It spoke of friendship and peace between the Lakota and the Americans, expressing lofty pledges. For example, Article I of the treaty states that "every injury or act of hostility, committed by one or either of the contracting parties against the other, shall be mutually forgiven and forgot." Article II declares that "there shall be perpetual peace and friendship between all the citizens of the United States, and all the individuals composing the aforesaid tribes [namely the Lakota]." Similar sentiments were expressed in a treaty signed between the Lakota and the United States in 1825.

Then, in 1837, the Lakota agreed to formally cede to the United States all the land that they had once inhabited east of the Mississippi River. By that year, the Lakota were no longer living in this territory since they had all migrated west into the plains. The Treaty of 1837 was thus a formal recognition of their changed life. In exchange for the land, the United States government made four promises to the Lakota. First, they gave the tribe $300,000 in initial payment. Second, they promised to provide annuities each year consisting of agricultural tools,

Lakota leaders meet with whites at Fort Laramie to discuss a peace treaty. This is the only known photograph of a Native American smoking a council pipe. The pipe was a sacred object, believed by the Lakota to have been given to them by the spirits as a means of communication with the spirit world.

mechanics' tools, and livestock. Third, the government offered to provide the Lakota with the services of a physician and a blacksmith. And fourth, they pledged to give an unspecified amount of provisions to the Lakota for a period of 20 years.

In contrast to treaties signed in the early part of the 19th century that essentially established friendship and goodwill between the Lakota and the United States, treaties of the later years resulted in major losses of land for the Lakota. The first such treaty, signed in 1851,

THE
CRISIS
CONTINUES

Just as the second half of the 18th century had been a turning point for the Teton, the second half of the 19th century was critical in the lives and history of Teton people. In the late 18th century, the Teton had expanded their economies and developed many of their cultural traditions. But in the late 19th century, they experienced numerous hardships and disasters. Most of their land was taken by the United States government, their traditional livelihood was destroyed, and their freedom of movement was denied. Thousands of Teton died, victims of brutal attacks by the American army and of devastating epidemic diseases that plagued their communities.

The half-century began with the signing of the first treaty of land cession in 1851. Then, during the 1850s and 1860s, warfare in the plains intensified as more American settlers made their way into the territory. The American army protected settlers and unleashed raids against the Teton and other American Indians who defended their homeland. Major wars erupted in Minnesota, the Dakotas, Nebraska, Kansas, and Colorado. As a result of constant turmoil and bloodshed experienced by the Teton, in 1868 they agreed to terms of an important treaty signed at Fort Laramie. In it, the Teton ceded much of the land that they controlled in South Dakota. They kept for themselves the territory between the Missouri River in the east, westward to the border of present-day South Dakota. This land, encompassing half of the state of South Dakota, was named the Great Sioux Reservation. The term *reservation* (*reserve* in Canada), which is widely used for American Indian land in North America, comes directly from wordings of many treaties between Native Americans and the U.S. government. In the treaties, American Indians agree to cede a specified portion of their original territory and "reserve for themselves" another specified amount of land. A "reservation" therefore consists of the land that the original inhabitants have "reserved for themselves." In exchange for land ceded by American Indians to the United States in treaties, the American government pledged to protect natives' rights to their reservations and to bar outsiders from encroaching on this territory.

In addition to defining the borders of the Great Sioux Reservation, the Treaty of 1868 stated that the U.S. government would give farm animals, equipment, and rations to the Teton. The government hoped that the Teton would give up their traditional way of life based on hunting buffalo in a vast open territory. American officials wanted the Teton, as well as other American Indians throughout the plains, to become farmers. These officials wanted American Indians to adopt the American style of rural living on small farms owned by individual families. They opposed native traditions that held that all land was controlled by the entire community, not by a single individual. And the government opposed native practices of traveling from place to place, hunting wild animals and gathering natural vegetation. They wanted American Indians to remain in one place so that they could be more easily supervised and controlled.

In keeping with these goals and in order to entice the Teton to conform to the officials' plans, the government promised to give 25,000 cows, 1,000 bulls, oxen, farming tools, and enough seeds for two years of planting. They also pledged to provide rations of beef, rice, flour, beans, sugar, coffee, and soap.

Finally, the Treaty of 1868 between the Teton and the United States mentioned the existence of "unceded Indian territory" which the Teton could use. American settlers were barred from encroaching on either the Teton reservation lands or "unceded Indian territory." Such pledges were soon broken.

When gold was discovered in the Black Hills of South Dakota in 1874, the government began to deny the Teton rights to their own land. The Black Hills were initially included in the territory possessed by the Teton as agreed in the Treaty of 1868. The Teton considered the Black Hills to be sacred land and were determined to keep it. But the discovery of gold lured many American prospectors, traders, and settlers into Teton land. Encroachment by Americans obviously violated terms of the treaty. In response to threats posed to Teton peace and survival, Teton warriors defended their communities and attacked the illegal settlements of Americans. And, as in the past, the United States government sent armies to protect the violators rather than to defend native people.

When the American government sent a delegation to the Teton in 1874 to try to buy the Black Hills for a sum of $6 million, the Teton refused. But more settlers and prospectors streamed into Teton territory. Cycles of American settlement, native defense of their land, and American military retaliation against the Teton continued. The army attacked other American Indian peoples as well. In some cases, the Teton helped defend other groups. For example, Oglala war-

Deadwood, a Gold Rush town in South Dakota, in 1876. A primary cause of the Great Sioux War of 1876 was the discovery by whites of gold in the Black Hills, which had been set aside by an earlier treaty as part of the Sioux reservation.

General George Armstrong Custer consults with some of his Native American scouts on the way to his ill-fated rendezvous with the Lakota and Cheyenne at the Little Bighorn on June 25, 1876.

riors under the leadership of the renowned Crazy Horse (1842–77) came to the aid of the Cheyenne when they were attacked by the army in 1876.

Some Americans living in eastern cities began to oppose the increasing conflict in the plains. They were disturbed by their own government's policies toward American Indians and were shocked by the deaths of thousands of innocent people in native communities. Leaders of the Teton and other Plains peoples were sometimes invited to speak to various organizations concerned with the plight of natives. For instance, the Teton leader Red Cloud traveled to New York City in 1871 to address members of the Cooper Institute. Red Cloud's impassioned speech stirred his audience to urge their government to bring about peace and justice for the Teton. Although the sentiments of some Americans were thus moved to support native peoples, their ideals did little to influence government policies.

Indeed, in March of 1876, the American government responded to the crisis created by intrusions of settlers into the plains by ordering the cavalry to round up all of the Lakota and force them to remain on their reservations. More pressure was put on the Teton to give up the sacred Black Hills. The commissioner of Indian affairs, Edward Smith, urged the Teton to sell the Black Hills "for the sake of promoting the mining and agricultural interests of white men." Commissioner Smith's statement clearly violated his supposed role as protector of American Indians' rights. Then, in 1877, fol-

lowing the Teton's continued refusal to sell, the United States Congress ignored the terms of the Treaty of 1868 and passed an act of Congress to confiscate the Black Hills from the Teton. Congress also unilaterally claimed that all "unceded Indian territory" named in the treaty belonged to the American government.

During the same period, some influential politicians and public figures put forth proposals to expel the Lakota from their reservations in South Dakota and force them to move to "Indian Territory" in the present-day state of Oklahoma. Although these suggestions were never put into operation, they revealed the attitude of many public officials concerning the government's power to ignore wishes and rights of American Indians.

And still the crisis continued. Indeed, it worsened. The American army and militias made up of American vigilantes attacked many native villages, killing the inhabitants and plundering their property. Soldiers and members of private militias were allowed to keep whatever goods they took from American Indians. One of the many accounts recalling the period has been given by the Oglala spiritual leader Black Elk. Black Elk described a raid commanded by Colonel Reynolds against an Oglala village led by Crazy Horse. The raid occurred on March 16, 1876:

> Crazy Horse stayed with about a
> hundred tepees on the Powder
> River. It was just daybreak. There was

a blizzard and it was very cold. The people were sleeping. Suddenly there were many shots and horses galloping through the village. It was the cavalry of the Wasichus [Americans], and they were yelling and shooting and riding their horses against the tepees. All the people rushed out and ran, because they were not awake yet and they were frightened. The soldiers killed as many women and children and men as they could while the people were running toward a bluff. Then they set fire to some of the tepees and knocked the others down. But when the people were on the side of the bluff, Crazy Horse said something, and all the warriors began singing the death song and charged back upon the soldiers; and the soldiers ran, driving many of the people's ponies ahead of them. Crazy Horse followed them all that day with a band of warriors, and that night he took all the stolen ponies away from them, and brought them back to the village.

The soldiers continued to come. In June of 1876, Oglala warriors defended their communities against renewed attacks by the American army. They stopped a cavalry unit in Montana that was headed for Teton territory. In response, the Americans sent a large expedition of 600 soldiers against the Teton. The army unit was led by General George Custer. Custer and his soldiers attacked a settlement of Teton people who were camped along the Little Bighorn River in South Dakota. Among the Teton was Sitting Bull (1834–90), the famed leader of the Hunkpapa Teton. During the ensuing battle between the Teton and Custer's soldiers, Teton warriors from other communities and warriors from other groups such as the Cheyenne came to defend native land and lives. In the end, the American Indians were victorious. They killed all of Custer's unit, including the general himself.

But the victory of the Teton and their allies did not stop the American army from continuing its attacks against American Indians. Seeking refuge and respite from the turmoil, Sitting Bull led his group into Canada. They hoped that conditions would improve and they would be able to return in peace. Sitting Bull later returned to South Dakota in 1881 and surrendered to the American government at Fort Buford, Montana, on July 19. He hoped, as others had before him, that peace would be established. But the tranquility he desired was not to be found.

After suffering numerous attacks, other Teton chiefs decided to surrender to the American government. They hoped that if they surrendered and renounced warfare, their people would be protected from further conflicts. In 1877, Crazy Horse agreed to go to Fort Robinson, Nebraska to meet with American officials in order to negotiate peace. But as soon as he arrived at the fort, he was arrested and imprisoned. Black Elk recounted the events of September 5, 1877:

> They told Crazy Horse they would not harm him if he would go and have

A Lakota depiction of the destruction of Custer's force at the Little Bighorn. The Lakota victory, however, only brought about a renewed determination on the part of the U.S. government to end their opposition and bring all bands onto the reservation.

This Lakota pictograph portrays the death of Crazy Horse while in custody at Fort Robinson, Nebraska, in 1877. A hero of the Indian victory at the Little Bighorn, Crazy Horse remains a revered hero of the Teton people.

a talk with the Wasichu chief there. But they lied. They did not take him to the chief for a talk. They took him to the little prison with iron bars on the windows, for they had planned to get rid of him. And when he saw what they were doing, he turned around and took a knife out of his robe and started out against all those soldiers. A soldier ran a bayonet into Crazy Horse from one side and he fell down and began to die.

The Oglala were to reside on the Pine Ridge Reservation; the Brulé at Rosebud; the Hunkpapa at Standing Rock; both the Miniconjou and the Itazipco at Cheyenne River; the Sihasapa at either Cheyenne River or Standing Rock; and the Oohenonpa at Cheyenne River and Rosebud.

Land on Teton reservations was alloted to separate families and individuals. By special terms of the Sioux Act, passed by Congress in 1889 to encourage the Teton to accept allotments, the usual allotment of 160 acres for each family was doubled so that every Teton head of household was assigned a total of 320 acres. Single individuals without families were given 80 acres of land. The remaining territory was open to claims from American settlers. After the policy of allotting land went into effect on February 10, 1890, the reservations carved from the Great Sioux Reservation together comprised approximately half of their original territory. The other half was sold to American settlers. Once again, terms of the Treaty of 1868 were directly violated by the American government.

The government further negated the treaty by threatening to cut off supplies of rations to the Teton when they continued to resist accepting allotments. Indeed, officials reduced by half the amount of rations given in the late 1880s and early 1890s. Many Teton lived on the brink of starvation and many died, owing both to lack of food and to general debilitation and malnutrition. Adding to the calamity, a severe drought occurred during the same period, resulting in the loss of crops grown by some Teton families.

Still, government officials were not content with only changing the economy of the Teton but also wanted to change the Teton's religious and cultural traditions. Programs aimed at managing the lives of American Indians were then designed by the federal Bureau of Indian Affairs. Although the bureau was established in part to protect American Indians' rights, officials often acted to undermine natives' freedom. During the 1870s, the bureau was headed by Thomas Morgan, commissioner of Indian affairs, who directed programs aimed at eradicating American Indians' traditional ways of life. The Teton, as well as other natives throughout the United States, were affected by Morgan's plans.

Teton religion and family life came under attack. Protestant and Catholic clergymen were sent to convert the Teton to Christianity. These missionaries preached against Teton beliefs and tried to persuade the people to give up their traditional ceremonies.

The government also sent teachers to set up boarding schools on the reservations. Teton children were forcibly separated from their families and housed in dormitories at boarding schools. They were not allowed to speak their own Lakota language. Teachers wanted to isolate children from their parents and communities so that they could be more easily indoctrinated into accepting American values. Even during summer-

Teton children in a music class taught by a white teacher. With the Lakota, as with other Native American peoples, the U.S. government used education as a tool of forcible assimilation.

time, when schools were not in session, children were not permitted to return to their families. Instead they were sent to work as domestics in the households of American settlers and government employees.

By 1890, the combination of many different government policies had a dev-astating effect on the Teton. Most of the territory they had once lived in had been taken from them, the buffalo they had hunted were gone forever, and their beliefs and ways of living were under constant attack. And so the people wondered if they would ever again be able to establish a good life for themselves.▲

Kicking Bear helped transmit the Ghost Dance religion to the Teton. Whites regarded the new religion, which proclaimed the imminent restoration of the Native American way of life, as an indication of a resurgent Indian militancy.

A
DREAM
DENIED

For many Teton, hopes for peace and prosperity were answered for a time in the promise of a new religion which was spreading among American Indians throughout western North America. The new religion was founded by a Paiute man named Wovoka (ca. 1860–1932) who lived in Nevada. It has become known as the Ghost Dance religion. Wovoka (also known by his English name, Jack Wilson) began the religion in 1889 after having a dramatic visionary experience during a total eclipse of the sun on January 1 of that year. In his vision, Wovoka was taken to heaven, where he saw God. God told him to return to earth and preach a message of peace and friendship. Wovoka urged American Indians to emphasize their traditional ways of relating to each other and to the world around them. He urged them to help one another, to be kind and generous to all. Wovoka said, "You must not fight. Do no harm to anyone. Do always right."

The Teton first heard of the new religion in 1889. They were told of it by more westerly groups such as the Arapaho and Shoshone. A delegation of Teton leaders traveled to Nevada late in 1889 to hear the message directly from Wovoka himself. The delegation included Good Thunder from the Pine Ridge Reservation, Short Bull from the Rosebud Reservation, and Kicking Bear from the Cheyenne River Reservation. In April of the following year, these men reported that they had met with Wovoka and that his words were good and true. The religion began to spread rapidly in all the Teton communities. People eagerly sought a message that gave them hope of a renewed life of harmony and well-being.

In addition to the moral principles that Wovoka emphasized, the Ghost Dance religion included a prophesy that the world as it then was would soon come to an end. The earth would tremble mightily, and after the cataclysm, only the American Indians would remain in North America. Everyone else would disappear. The prophesy also predicted that all the American Indians who had died would return and rejoin their families and friends. And buffalo would return to roam the plains and prairies in great numbers as they had done in prior times. The life that native people had once known before the arrival of Europeans would be restored.

In order to prepare for this event, believers of the new religion conducted ceremonies and dances of celebration and hope. Each tribe performed the rites in its own way, often adding to or elaborating specific themes and performing its special songs and dances.

Many Teton rites began with the following song expressing belief in the return of the dead:

> The father says so.
> The father says so.
> You shall see your grandfather.
> The father says so.
> You shall see your kindred.
> The father says so.

Individuals often composed their own songs, some of which became widely popular with all Teton worshipers. The following song was composed by a young woman who encountered a vision of her deceased mother:

> Mother, come home; mother, come home.
> My little brother goes about always crying,

My little brother goes about always crying.
Mother, come home; mother, come home.

Another Teton song expressed themes of renewal and restoration of past ways of living:

> The whole world is coming,
> A nation is coming, a nation is coming.
> The Eagle has brought the message to the tribe.
> The father says so, the father says so.
> Over the whole earth, they are coming.
> The buffalo are coming, the buffalo are coming.
> The Crow has brought the message to the tribe.
> The father says so, the father says so.

Rituals of the Ghost Dance religion included prayers and offerings to spirits as well as songs and dances celebrating the return of the dead and restoration of a renewed life. Descriptions of ceremonies were occasionally made by Americans who had contact with Teton believers. J. F. Asay, an American trader living at the Pine Ridge agency, described one ritual that took place in 1890:

> The dancers first stood in line facing the sun, while the leader, standing facing them, made a prayer and waved over their heads the "ghost stick," a staff about six feet long, trimmed with red cloth and feathers of the same color. After thus waving

Wovoka (left), known also as Jack Wilson, was the Paiute prophet who preached the Ghost Dance religion and came to be known as the Messiah to those who believed in his message of renewal.

A pictograph of costumes worn by the Ghost Dancers. By dancing and performing other ceremonial rituals, the Ghost Dancers could hasten the return of the old world they had known before the arrival of Europeans. The shirts worn by the figures at center and at right were supposed to protect the practitioners of the religion from the bullets of the white men.

the stick over them, he faced the sun and made another prayer, after which the line closed up to form a circle around the tree [which had been placed in the dance ground] and the dance began. During the prayer a woman standing near the tree held out a pipe toward the sun, while another beside her held out four arrows from which the points had been removed.

Participants then proceeded to sing and dance. As they did so, they often saw visions of their deceased relatives and received messages from the spirit world.

Not surprisingly, the message of return and renewal had great appeal to people devastated by warfare, poverty, starvation, and disease. They listened to words of hope spoken to them and participated in dances and songs dedicated to achieving the dream of peace and prosperity.

And not surprisingly, the American government and settlers were alarmed by the prophesy predicting their disappearance. But American farmers and ranchers invented and exaggerated the danger posed to them by adherents of the Ghost Dance religion. They imagined that American Indians would descend upon their communities, hastening their demise. Such attacks were in no way a part of the religion. Ghost Dance participants never organized raids against settlers. But settlers' fears were aroused and used to enflame hostility against the Teton and other native peoples.

Government officials often added to the already tense situation by advocating military action against believers in the Ghost Dance religion. For instance, a man named Royer who headed the Bureau of Indian Affairs' agency at the Pine Ridge Reservation wrote to his superiors in Washington, D.C., on October 30, 1890:

> Your Department has been informed of the damage resulting from these dances and of the danger attending them of the crazy Indians doing serious damage to others. I have carefully studied the matter and have brought all the persuasion to bear on the leaders that was possible but without effect and the only remedy for this matter is the use of military and until this is done you need not expect any progress from these people on the other hand you will be made to realize that they are tearing down more in a day than the Government can build in a month.

Another federal agent, James McLaughlin, in charge of the BIA's office on the Standing Rock Reservation, told Sitting Bull that the Ghost Dance religion was "absurd." He said that Sitting Bull should stop people at Standing Rock from participating in the dances. Sitting Bull responded by suggesting that both he and McLaughlin travel to Nevada to hear Wovoka's message directly from the man himself. Sitting Bull said that if the doctrine was false, he would do whatever he could to persuade his people to ignore it. But McLaughlin refused. Instead, on November 19, 1890, he asked officials of the BIA to allow him to withhold rations from people remaining in Sitting Bull's village at Standing Rock. Only those people who moved to the agency's grounds would be given food to eat. Most people did not comply even under the threat of starvation in the bitter winter already underway.

In response to growing fears on the part of Americans living in former Teton territory, the government outlawed the Teton's participation in Ghost Dances. From time to time, soldiers were sent to break up dances and arrest those people deemed responsible for leading them. In November 1890, President Harrison gave the secretary of war instructions to "suppress any threatened outbreak" of the Ghost Dance.

This order was immediately put into effect. On November 20, 1890, more than 1,000 U.S. troops entered the Pine Ridge and Rosebud reservations. They set up guards around agency offices and government installations, including the Oglala boarding school at Pine Ridge. Children in the school, numbering a hundred, were not permitted to leave nor were their parents allowed to enter.

Tensions at Pine Ridge, Standing Rock, and surrounding communities

James McLaughlin (center) was the agent in charge of the Standing Rock reservation, where Sitting Bull held out as a symbol of defiance of the white man. It was McLaughlin who in 1890 ordered Sitting Bull's arrest, which ended in the great leader's death and indirectly set in motion the events that resulted in the massacre at Wounded Knee.

increased during the next few weeks. Then, on December 15, James McLaughlin, the agent at Standing Rock, ordered the arrest of Sitting Bull. Police came at dawn to Sitting Bull's cabin at Standing Rock and tried to arrest him. His supporters were also present. Shots rang out from both sides. Sitting Bull was killed by one of the policemen. Others, both Teton and American, also were shot and killed.

Troops were soon ordered by General Nelson Miles, commander of the army in Lakota territory, to arrest another Teton leader named Big Foot. Big Foot was a chief of the Miniconjou band of Teton. He was well known as a

peaceful man and as a negotiator between the Teton and American officials. But, he too became a victim in the developing storm stirred by fears and exaggerations. When Big Foot was invited by other Teton leaders to come to the agency at Pine Ridge in order to help negotiate a peaceful resolution of the crisis, he was intercepted by soldiers under the command at Fort Bennet. Big Foot was ordered to go to the fort but he decided to continue his trip to Pine Ridge to negotiate peace. Big Foot and his followers set up their camp at Wounded Knee Creek on December 28, 1890. The group consisted of approximately 120 men and 230 women and

(continued on page 81)

THE
SACRED
AND THE
MUNDANE

On this page and the seven that follow it, various items of Teton Lakota material culture are displayed. Ranging from articles of war to items of clothing, from everyday conveniences to children's playthings, the artifacts are united in their combination of the ceremonial with the quotidian, the beautiful and the functional. In that regard they are superb representatives of traditional Teton Lakota culture, which imbued the workings of the natural world and virtually every aspect of human behavior with spiritual significance. For the Lakota, as for many other Native American peoples, there was no distance between "religious" and "everyday" life: the world was a place of infinite mystery and spiritual power, which the people were obligated to honor and respect. The ornamentation on such items as a pair of moccasins or a child's rattle are thus not merely decorative but representations of the sacred and reminders to the people of their place in the world.

Representations of a black buffalo with a fish on its side, two small birds, and a crane adorn the head of this Teton Lakota drum obtained by Mary Collins, a Christian missionary who lived with the Teton in the late 19th century.

The various pictographs on this Teton woman's dress, thought to date from 1840 to 1860, are believed to record either images from her dreams or her husband's exploits in battle.

This Teton child's moccasins are made of buckskin, with colored quills and beads used to create the tipi design on the vamp.

The beaded geometric designs on this pair of Teton moccasins for an adult male are intended as a representation of the four winds. According to anthropologist Ruth Underhill, "the nomadic Sioux . . . paid particular attention to the directions, the home of the four winds. Every object and every movement in a ceremony was oriented either toward the West, home of the buffalo; or the North, that of the purifying cold wind; or the East, whence wisdom comes; or the South, the warm country 'towards which we always face.'"

75

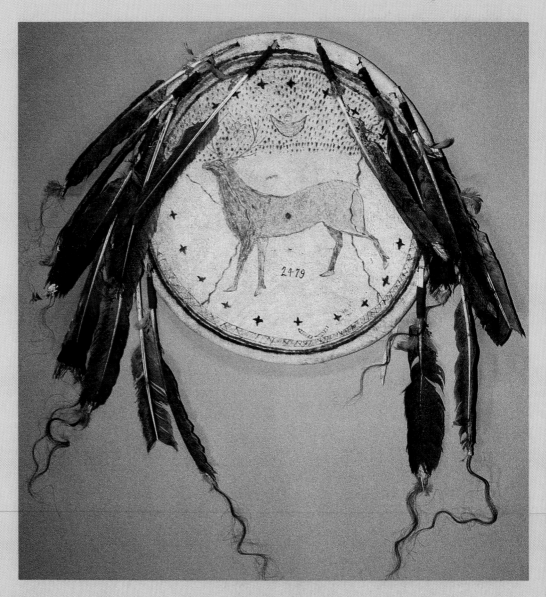

The two shields on these pages were intended for use in ceremonial dances rather than as protection in warfare. This shield, with pictographs of the night sky, rattlesnakes, a spider, a person, and an elk, probably belonged to a member of the Elk Dreamer society.

This shield was made for ceremonial use by a Teton named Fat Bear in the late 19th century. It was made from buckskin stretched over a rawhide frame; the attached feathers are from an eagle.

This vest and pants were intended for wear by a Teton boy. They date from approximately 1890.

This small bag was used to carry tinder and material with which to start a fire.

The geometric designs on this Teton child's turtle fetish represent the four winds. The torso of the turtle was made of buckskin; the legs were made of rawhide and sewn to the body with animal sinew.

These buckskin tipi bags were used as all-purpose carriers by the Teton Lakota. They date from approximately 1895 and feature a common beaded design of various geometric shapes.

(continued from page 72)

children. They were immediately surrounded by the American army. The next day, December 29, Big Foot and his people were told to give up all of their guns. Most did so, but some still held on to their weapons. The confrontation became more intense. Shots rang out from the soldiers and from the Teton defending themselves. The army responded by massacring the people. Over 300 were killed, later to be buried in a mass grave. Two-thirds of the victims were women and children. Big Foot also died in the attack. One eyewitness to the tragedy, a Teton man named Turning Hawk, later described the scene:

All the men who were in a bunch were killed right there, and those who escaped that first fire got into the ravine, and as they went along up the ravine for a long distance they were pursued on both sides by the soldiers and shot down, as the dead bodies showed afterwards. The women were standing off at a different place from where the men were stationed, and when the firing began, those of the men who escaped the first onslaught went in one direction up the ravine, and then the women, who were bunched together at another place, went entirely in a different direction through an open field, and the women fared the same fate as the men who went up the deep ravine.

Another witness, American Horse, added more details:

An Oglala encampment at Pine Ridge, one of the reservations, along with Rosebud, where the Teton adherents of the Ghost Dance religion were generally located.

Big Foot lies dead in the snow at Wounded Knee in December 1890. Around him lay the bodies of more than 250 members of the Miniconjou band, many of them women and children.

The women as they were fleeing with
their babies were killed together,
shot right through, and the women
who were very heavy with child
were also killed. All the Indians fled,
and after most all of them had been
killed a cry was made that those who
were not killed or wounded should
come forth and they would be safe.
Little boys who were not wounded
came out of their places of refuge, and
as soon as they came in sight a
number of soldiers surrounded them
and butchered them there.

When other Teton residing at Pine Ridge heard news of the massacre, they fled the area for fear that they too would be killed. Soon thereafter, most of the Teton returned and their leaders surrendered to government authorities. The last Teton chief to surrender was Kicking Bear. He finally gave in to the power of the United States on January 15, 1891.

The tragic events that occurred at Wounded Knee aroused enough outrage on the part of some influential Americans to call for an official investigation into the massacre. These calls led to the public hearing for the first time about the deplorable living conditions of the Teton people. Inquiries were held in 1891 to hear testimony and receive reports from government officials, missionaries, and army officers who described life for the Teton. In one account, General Miles noted that the Lakota had

signed away a valuable portion of
their reservation, and it is now
occupied by white people, for which
they [the Lakota] have received
nothing. They understood that ample
provision would be made for their
support; instead, their supplies have
been reduced and much of the time
they have been living on half and two-
thirds rations. The disaffection is
widespread. These facts are beyond
question, and the evidence is
positive and sustained by thousands
of witnesses.

Miles quoted from a report written by the commander of Fort Yates in North Dakota concerning the Teton living at Standing Rock. The report listed numerous failures of the United States government contributing to the poverty and demoralization of the people. Among them:

Failure of the government to provide
the full allowance of seeds and
agricultural implements to Indians
engaged in farming.

Failure of the government to issue such Indians the full number of cows and oxen.

Failure of the government to issue to the Indians the full amount of annuity supplies to which they are entitled.

Failure of the government to have the clothing and other annuity supplies ready for issue.

Failure of the government to appropriate money for the payment of the Indians for the ponies taken from them.

The commander concluded that:

It appears that the government has failed to fulfill its obligations, and in order to render the Indians law-abiding, peaceful, contented, and prosperous it is strongly recommended that the treaties be promptly and fully carried out, and that the promises made be faithfully kept.

In another report, Captain J. H. Hurst, commander of Fort Bennet in South Dakota, detailed numerous complaints voiced by the Teton. They included:

(1) That the boundaries of the reservation are not what they agreed to;
(2) That they have never received full recompense for the ponies taken from them;
(3) That the game has been destroyed and driven out of the country by the white people;
(4) That their children are taken from them and kept for years [at boarding schools] instead of being educated among them;
(5) That the rations issued to them are insufficient in quantity and frequently very poor in quality.

Finally, Bishop W. H. Hare, an Episcopal minister living at Pine Ridge, said that starvation, lack of annuity supplies, and rampant epidemics of measles, whooping cough, and influenza had decimated the population at Pine Ridge and the other Teton reservations.

In the context of life as described in written and oral testimony, many Teton had responded by seeking relief in the hope given by the Ghost Dance religion's message of spiritual power, moral renewal, and restoration of an earlier way of living. But the American government responded by subjecting the Teton to further deprivation. And the army responded with increased military force.

The massacre of innocent people at Wounded Knee Creek on December 29, 1890, has come to be a symbol of the plight of native people all over North America. The people's hope for a new life and their dream of harmony and justice were answered with brutal death, buried in a mass grave.

But still the Teton survived. Their will to endure remained strong as they faced new challenges, accepting changes in their lives but also determined to maintain their own cultural traditions. ▲

Lakota cowboys brand cattle on the Pine Ridge reservation in the early 20th century. For a time on the reservation, cattle ranching seemed as if it might provide a means of self-support for the Lakota, but the federal government's policies proved extremely counter-productive to Teton ranchers.

SEEKING
A
NEW
WAY

In the early years of the 20th century, the Teton began a slow process of adopting a new lifestyle. Their faith in their own traditions remained strong but they also realized that the old ways were gone forever. Economic and political changes were forced upon them by the United States government and its agencies. In this context, the people sought to establish a life for themselves that incorporated necessary changes but was true to their own values.

At the turn of the century, even after many years of government pressure, most Teton had not accepted individual allotments. They preferred to hold their land communally. But within a few decades, the Bureau of Indian Affairs succeeded in dividing all of the Teton reservations into allotted shares. The policy was disastrous for several reasons. First, after allotments were assigned to each family, the remaining land was declared "surplus" and was sold either to the U.S. government or to American farmers and ranchers. This process resulted in a loss of millions of acres.

Second, more land was lost when individual owners were permitted to sell their land. According to procedures outlined by the Dawes Act of 1887, allotted land was held in trust for a period of 25 years. An owner could not sell his or her land during that time but could do so after the trust period ended. Many Teton people did agree to sell their land, some out of ignorance or from trickery and some because of dire poverty and the need to have money to support themselves.

A final unfortunate result of allotment policies stemmed from procedures concerning inheritance of land. Since ownership passes to all descendants, some pieces of land are now owned by over a hundred people. Decisions about how to use the land often involve many owners and become so complicated that nothing is done.

All of the Teton reservations have suffered from these various effects of allotment policies. Loss of land is the most significant problem, because without land, the people lose any possibility of economic development and prosperity. For example, by 1934, the Rosebud Reservation had lost 2,195,905 acres of its original territory. Most of this land was sold to outsiders, although some was ceded to the U.S. government. A second example concerns the Pine Ridge Reservation which originally contained 2,721,597 acres of land. During the years between 1904 and 1916, a total of 8,275 individual plots, amounting to 2,380,195 acres, were assigned. The "surplus" land of 182,653 acres was sold to the U.S. government. Only about 147,000 acres remained under tribal ownership. Since then, more than half of the land in allotments has gone out of native control. Some has been sold and the rest leased to outside farmers and ranchers. The Teton therefore currently control less than half of their reservation territory.

Still, despite these serious problems, many Teton people were able to prosper. By the time of World War I, the Oglala at Pine Ridge had successfully developed large herds of cattle. They also raised many horses and were breeders of some of the best horses in North America. Since these enterprises were communally controlled, all of the people benefitted. Then, in 1917, after the United States entered World War I, the BIA agent in charge of Pine Ridge sold all of the Oglala's cattle on the pretext that they were needed for the war effort. Rangeland on which the Oglala's cattle

had formerly grazed was then leased to non-Indian cattle herders.

After the war ended, more land was leased to outsiders. Large American agricultural companies were expanding their acreage and succeeded in persuading the BIA to allow leasing of land on Teton reservations to their enterprises.

And so the Teton continued to lose access to their own land. As a result, the population on the reservations gradually became split into two groups. One group of people retained control of their land and continued to make their living from farming and ranching. The other group consisted of landless people who migrated to agency towns on the reservations. There they sought work to support themselves. But since the only work available in towns was connected to the federal government, these people became dependent on the BIA agent and other officials for their jobs.

Federal policy toward American Indians began to change in the 1930s in the context of New Deal policies promoted by President Franklin D. Roosevelt. At that time, the commissioner of Indian affairs, John Collier, developed a new program aimed at changing the relations between American Indians and the federal government. Collier's policies were, in part, a response to a national report on living conditions on reservations throughout the United States. The report, called the Meriam Report, after its principal writer, was issued in 1928 after several years of intensive research. The Meriam Report

A homesteading expedition searches for claims in the Dakota Territory in 1887. That same year, the Dawes Act divided communally held Indian land into privately owned allotments. Subsequently, many Native Americans lost their land to settlers and commercial interests.

reviewed living conditions, health status, educational programs and achievements, and governing structures on American Indian reservations. After reviewing the evidence, the report vigorously condemned the Dawes Act of 1887 and the ensuing policies of the federal government. It condemned the breakup of American Indians' territory and shrinkage of their land base. It noted the deplorable living conditions and health status endured by native peoples. And it criticized the educational system which forced American Indian children to leave their families and communities to be taught in boarding schools.

John Collier, appointed Commissioner of Indian Affairs by President Franklin Roosevelt, is remembered by many Native Americans as a relatively sympathetic federal official.

The Meriam Report made significant recommendations to reorient federal policy. It urged ending the boarding school system and replacing it with an extensive network of day schools on reservations. It also urged that tribal groups themselves have more power to make decisions concerning programs and policies affecting their communities. And the Meriam Report stressed the right of American Indians to maintain their language and cultural traditions if they chose to do so.

Influenced by findings and recommendations of the Meriam Report, John

Collier's efforts to revamp government policy culminated in passage by Congress of the Indian Reorganization Act (IRA) of 1934. The act principally provided for establishment of limited self-government on reservations. Each reservation was able to adopt a tribal constitution and set up a tribal council based on elections by members of the tribe. These councils were given responsibility to manage federal and local programs operating on their reservations. They were given authority to develop economic resources as tribal enterprises. And they had the task of helping to manage and carry out efforts at improving living standards, health, and education for their people.

Collier was also able to convince Congress to appropriate funds for two special projects. Two million dollars per year were to be spent on purchasing new land adjacent to reservations in order to restore at least some of the territory lost through treaty violations. And five million dollars per year were granted for programs of economic development and educational improvement on reservations.

In accordance with the IRA's provisions, the Teton reservations adopted tribal constitutions and established councils in 1935. This shift to self-government has been beneficial in its emphasis on local control and local decision making. However, previous problems stemming from loss of access to land have continued and, indeed, increased. Many landless people have now become dependent for their jobs on patronage from members of tribal councils. Political control by a few over many has therefore only shifted from BIA agents to local tribal councils.

Divisions between rural dwellers and townspeople have grown sharper. These splits are not only of residence but also involve differences in attitudes toward Teton life. Rural residents tend to retain their use of the native Lakota language and to be involved in traditional religious, social, and cultural events. In contrast, townspeople tend to speak English and adopt other facets of American culture.

Despite these significant differences, though, all the Teton are faced with many of the same problems. As a tribe, issues concerning land and its use have remained paramount. Their territory, although guaranteed by treaties, continues to be in jeopardy. For example, when the federal government built an extensive system of dams along the Missouri River in the late 1940s and early 1950s, land on two Teton reservations was flooded in the process. The Standing Rock Reservation and the Cheyenne River Reservation lost most of their arable and wooded land. One dam in particular, the Oahe Dam, flooded 160,889 acres of the best rangeland and farms on the reservations. Nearly all of their timber resources and wild fruit areas were also destroyed.

The need to develop tribal economies and provide jobs for residents continues to be a major concern of the Teton. Federal policies have sometimes undermined their efforts to establish thriving enterprises on the reservations. Sale of their successful cattle herds during World War I and destruction of their most valuable farmland and timber resources in the building of dams took away much of the income generated by the Teton. As a result, levels of unemployment were extremely high, reaching as much as 70 percent. And without independent economic ventures to produce jobs, half of those people who work on the reservations are employed by federal or local government organizations.

As a response to widespread poverty on American Indian reservations

COME TO DENVER.

THE CHANCE OF YOUR LIFETIME !

Good Jobs
Retail Trade
Manufacturing
Government-Federal, State, Local
Wholesale Trade
Construction of Buildings, Etc.

Happy Homes
Beautiful Houses
Many Churches
Exciting Community Life
Over Half of Homes Owned by Residents
Convenient Stores-Shopping Centers

Training
Vocational Training
Auto Mech., Beauty Shop, Drafting,
Nursing, Office Work, Watchmaking
Adult Education
Evening High School, Arts and Crafts
Job Improvement, Home-making

Beautiful Colorado
"Tallest" State, 48 Mt. Peaks Over 14,000 Ft.
350 Days Sunshine, Mild Winters
Zoos, Museums, Mountain Parks, Drives
Picnic Areas, Lakes, Amusement Parks
Big Game Hunting, Trout Fishing, Camping

Advertisements such as this one were used to persuade Native Americans to participate in the Bureau of Indian Affairs' relocation program. The program was an attempt to encourage economic advancement and cultural assimilation by convincing Native Americans to move off the reservations into various urban areas.

throughout the country, the Bureau of Indian Affairs instituted a new policy in the 1940s aimed at encouraging American Indians to leave their reservations and move to cities where jobs were supposedly available. Through the so-called relocation program, the government provided funds to pay for transportation to a city and in some cases to help pay the fees for job-training instruction. Although some Teton agreed to relocate

to such cities as Rapid City, South Dakota; Minneapolis, Minnesota; Green Bay, Wisconsin; and Denver, Colorado, most chose to remain in their home communities where they continued to have the social support of their families and friends. And for those people who did relocate, many returned when they found that few jobs were actually available for them. Without jobs, they had often ended up living in poor urban ghettos.

During the 1960s, programs related to President Lyndon Johnson's "War on Poverty" provided an influx of jobs on Teton reservations. However, access to these jobs was often dependent on the old system of patronage, through which positions were given out by members of tribal councils. The power of councillors thus increased during this period.

The Teton were affected by other trends alive in the 1960s as well. Many American Indians throughout North America became involved in political organizations aimed at strengthening native rights and safeguarding provisions guaranteed in treaties. Issues of maintaining and restoring land originally within reservation boundaries and of hunting and fishing rights were especially important. Many Teton and other Lakota became very active in promoting goals of native organizations. Some took part in efforts to bring local and national attention to the needs of American Indians. For example, in 1964, after the federal government closed a prison on Alcatraz Island in San Francisco Bay and declared the land "excess property," a number of Teton living in San Francisco filed a suit in court to claim the island. Although their suit was dismissed, the action brought attention to questions of land ownership and control that are vitally important to native peoples.

The claim of the Lakota in San Francisco laid the groundwork for a major action in November 1969, when more than a hundred American Indians from all over the United States took over the prison grounds on Alcatraz Island. Since the San Francisco American Indian Center had recently burned down, the people asked that the island be used as a site for a new American Indian community center. The group of activists formed an organization called Indians of All Tribes,

In March 1964, a delegation of Teton Lakota occupied the island of Alcatraz, off the coast of San Francisco, as a gesture of protest to call attention to Native American land claims.

Hundreds of Native American protesters occupied the Bureau of Indian Affairs building in Washington, D.C., in November 1972 as part of the American Indian Movement's Trail of Broken Treaties.

stressing the mutual problems facing all native peoples. They remained on the island for 19 months. In the end, they were evicted by U.S. marshals. However, during the occupation, the group was able to bring national attention to conditions and concerns of American Indians.

In addition to participating in many native organizations and activities, several Teton men were among the founders of one of the most militant American Indian rights groups, the American Indian Movement (AIM). AIM began in 1968 among urban American Indians living in Minneapolis, Minnesota. Its founders were Russell Means, Dennis Banks, both Teton, and two Chippewa brothers, Vernon and Clyde Bellancourt. AIM's goals were similar to those of other native rights organizations, but their methods were sometimes more confrontational. Members of AIM believed that it was often necessary to publicly confront people who held political power, both on reservations and in the state and federal systems. They organized demonstrations to arouse the public, both locally and nationally, concerning conditions faced by American

Indians in the United States. Issues related to legal rights, treaty obligations, and land losses were of major concern.

AIM members took part in a national demonstration in 1972 called the Trail of Broken Treaties. This effort was planned to focus attention on the long history of the government's failure to keep promises it made in treaties with American Indians. Loss of land, violation of treaty obligations, and denial of native rights were all issues brought before the public as American Indian marchers walked from Seattle to Washington, D.C. They ended their march at the offices of the Bureau of Indian Affairs in the nation's capital. There they barricaded themselves in the BIA building and pledged to remain until their demands were addressed. They stayed for six days, reviewing files and releasing documents that they said showed the agency's negligence in carrying out its supposed goal of protecting American Indians' rights.

During 1972, several local events occurred that had an immediate impact on people in Teton communities. One was the murder of Raymond Yellow Thunder, an Oglala man from Pine Ridge. He was set upon by two men in Gordon, Nebraska, who stripped him of his clothes and forced him to enter an American Legion hall where a dance was in progress. Then he was beaten so severely that he died of his injuries. But his tormentors and killers were only charged with second degree manslaughter instead of murder. They served one year in jail for their crime. People at Pine Ridge and the other Teton reservations,

as well as Teton living in urban areas in South Dakota, were outraged by the murder of Yellow Thunder and by the light punishment meted out to his killers. They organized demonstrations in Nebraska of over 2,000 people to protest the system of justice that treats Native American offenders harshly but treats leniently those who commit crimes against natives.

A second important event of 1972 was the founding of the Oglala Sioux Civil Rights Organization at Pine Ridge. The founders were disturbed by what they saw as corruption and abuse of power by local tribal leaders. This issue stemmed from the long-standing problem of control over tribal affairs wielded by tribal councillors and the tribal president. In 1972, a bitter election campaign for president of the tribal council took place between Gerald One Feather and Richard Wilson. One Feather represented the more traditional residents of Pine Ridge who were keenly interested in preserving Teton cultural traditions and ways of living. Wilson represented the townspeople who tended to be more oriented toward American values and lifestyles. The contest between One Feather and Wilson symbolized the split in ideology between rural and town dwellers in the Teton population.

Wilson won the election and immediately attempted to block activities of his opponents. He persuaded the tribal council to ban the AIM organization from the Pine Ridge Reservation. Then he formed an Oglala police force to help enforce the ban. The two primary found-

Russell Means (left) and Dennis Banks, two of the leaders of the American Indian Movement (AIM), speak with the press at Wounded Knee, on the Pine Ridge reservation, in March 1973. The leaders and supporters of AIM had occupied Wounded Knee several days earlier, resulting in a 71-day, sometime-violent standoff with federal law enforcement officials.

ers of AIM, Russell Means and Dennis Banks, became particular targets of Wilson's campaign.

As could be expected, Wilson's policies highlighted and intensified divisions among people at Pine Ridge. His supporters said that his actions were necessary to maintain peace on the reservation and to keep "outside agitators" from disrupting the community. Wilson's opponents said that he abused his power in order to punish anyone who disagreed with him. They claimed that the reservation police force acted like a "goon squad," mistreating and physically beating Wilson's opponents.

Then, in February of 1973, some of the tribal councillors from Pine Ridge formed a group called the Inter-District Council of the Oglala Sioux Tribe. They opposed Wilson's tactics, stating that he was corrupt and abusive. Three of the councillors filed proceedings to impeach Wilson. Wilson responded by declaring a state of emergency on the reservation and calling in U.S. marshals to keep the peace.

Later that month, several traditional leaders at Pine Ridge met to discuss the developing crisis. They decided to invite Russell Means and other members of AIM to come to the reservation and help protect their rights. AIM had previously expressed interest not only in safeguarding native rights guaranteed by treaties with the federal government but in fighting corruption in tribal politics as well. Its willingness to confront local politicians and power brokers brought it to the attention of the people at Pine

Ridge who sought to preserve Teton traditions. After the meeting between AIM and the supporters of traditional ways, Dennis Banks recalled that two of the women made desperate pleas for AIM's support. Banks remembered the words of Helen Moves Camp:

> She started to cry during her talk to me. She came right up to me, crying, and she was begging for help. She said that if it's the last thing we do, we should fight for Indian people, and fight there.

According to Helen Moves Camp's recollections, the chiefs then suggested that AIM members go to the village of Wounded Knee on the Pine Ridge Reservation and make their protest there. Banks, Means, and the other AIM members agreed and on February 27 proceeded to Wounded Knee, stopping at the site of the mass grave of victims of the Wounded Knee massacre of 1890. One of the protesters, a spiritual leader named Leonard Crow Dog, offered a prayer at the site and said:

> Here we come going the other way. It's just like those Indian soldiers in Big Foot's band who were going to Pine Ridge, and now they're coming back. We're those soldiers, we're those Indian people, we're them, we're back, and we can't go any further.

Returning to Wounded Knee in 1973 to bring attention to the problems of Teton people made use of the powerful symbol of the oppression of American

Modern-day Teton warriors stand guard outside the Church of the Sacred Heart in the course of AIM's occupation of Wounded Knee.

Indians in North America. The feelings of participants were expressed by Dennis Banks:

> We all knew when he [Leonard Crow Dog] got done talking that we would have to do or die at Wounded Knee. Everything pointed to one course of action—retake Wounded Knee. The medicine men brought wisdom to us. They gave us the spiritual direction we needed. There was no writing letters to the government and sending them demands any more. That's exactly what the medicine men said to us— "when you put your words on paper, then they step on them." So the direction that we received was good.

As news of the occupation of Wounded Knee spread throughout the United States, hundreds of native and nonnative supporters came to Pine Ridge. Within a few weeks, 300 American Indians were barricaded in the village, determined to remain until the federal government responded to their demands. They called on the government to investigate activities and policies of the BIA and to adhere to promises made in treaties with American Indians. They also wanted the Oglala to be free to decide their own form of local government instead of being forced to comply with federal policies.

The protesters were surrounded by a force of 300 federal marshals, FBI agents, and police officers. From time to time, the confrontation erupted into gunfire. By the end of the 71-day occupation, two American Indians had been killed and two were wounded. One federal marshal was also wounded.

Russell Means, Dennis Banks, and more than 30 other demonstrators were charged with a variety of felonies in connection with the occupation, but they were acquitted because of illegal actions taken by the government in pursuing the case. Such actions included use of illegal wiretaps, paid witnesses, altered evidence, and the perjuring of prosecution witnesses.

And so the community at Wounded Knee became, for a second time, the symbol of American Indians' hopes for a future free from interference from government authorities. The hope remains.▲

"Black Hills Bob" Humphrey (left) stands with Russell Means outside his encampment in the Black Hills in November 1981. Humphrey and other Teton activists were camped in the hills to call attention to the Lakota's continuing campaign to regain control of the Black Hills. Land rights continue to be one of the most important issues for modern-day Native Americans.

THE
TETON
TODAY

The Teton today face many of the same problems as they did in past years— indeed in past centuries. They strive to retain their territory, to seek justice for their people, and to maintain a harmonious community life. They seek a balance between the changes experienced by all people in the world today and the values derived from their own traditions.

The Teton continue to be embroiled in controversies concerning land and legal rights. For more than a century, they have struggled to regain possession of the Black Hills, taken from them by an act of Congress in 1877. The issue remains important to the Teton because it represents a long history of illegal actions by the government against their people. And many Teton consider the Black Hills to be sacred land, inhabited by powerful spirits.

After congressional hearings were held in 1974 regarding the Teton's claim for the Black Hills, the Teton were awarded a sum of $17.5 million as compensation for the land. They were also given $85 million in interest payments. The Department of Justice objected to the settlement and appealed to the Court of Claims, a court established to hear cases involving American Indians' land claims. In 1980, the court awarded the Teton a total of $105 million. This ruling was upheld by the Supreme Court.

Despite a favorable monetary judgment, the Teton have refused to accept payment in exchange for title to the Black Hills. Instead, they want the territory returned to them. Their continued claims to the region are based on both the Treaty of 1868 and the American Indian Freedom of Religion Act, which Congress passed in 1978. They have appealed to Senator Daniel Inouye, chair of the Senate Committee on Indian Affairs, to settle the case. The matter is still pending. Meanwhile, the money awarded to the Teton remains in trust in a BIA account, collecting interest.

A second lingering legal controversy concerns the case of Leonard Peltier. Peltier, an Oglala activist from Pine Ridge, was involved in an incident that occurred in 1975 in Custer, South Dakota. Details remain uncertain, but an exchange of gunfire took place between several Oglala men and four FBI agents. Two of the agents and one Oglala man were killed. Leonard Peltier and three other Oglalas were arrested and charged with murder. Two of the men were put on trial first and both were acquitted. Peltier decided to seek refuge in Canada rather than stand trial because he believed that he would not get a fair hearing. After his extradition from Canada, which was protested by many members of the Canadian parliament, Peltier was tried, convicted, and sentenced to life imprisonment.

Peltier and his lawyers have since appealed the verdict and requested a new trial based on evidence they have uncovered showing the government's illegal activities in investigating and prosecuting the case. Among these are the tampering of evidence, suppression of ballistics reports, and coercion of prosecution witnesses. Requests for a new trial have been repeatedly denied by the courts, but appeals continue to be filed. Peltier's requests are supported by letters from many members of Congress, by a number of religious leaders throughout the world, and by Amnesty International, a prominent human rights organization which has declared Peltier to be a political prisoner of conscience.

Although issues such as the Black Hills land claim and the Peltier case have gained national and even international attention, the Teton are also faced with problems in their home communities. High rates of unemployment, lack of capital to invest in economic enterprises, and poor health-care services continue to be major problems.

But the Teton continue to attempt to find solutions to their difficulties, merging new methods with age-old traditions. Participation in community events which express Teton values of harmony, generosity, and cooperation help sustain the people. One such event is the giveaway. A giveaway is a traditional ceremonial distribution of gifts. In prior times, it occurred at the end of a one-year period of mourning after a death. A year's mourning, called Keeping of the Soul, is one of the Teton's Seven Sacred Rites. At giveaways, relatives of the deceased distributed goods to people in the community. Goods of many types were given, but horses and buffalo robes were especially prized.

Today, giveaways are held to mark many important occasions including births, marriages, and graduations. People now give quilts, clothing, and household goods to their guests.

Although the occasions for giveaways and the items distributed have changed, the underlying values expressed by the event remain the same. Gifts are given in order to establish lasting bonds of friendship and cooperation with others. Individuals give to others as a real and symbolic way of showing that they value sharing and generosity. Through acts of giving, they expand the network of people with whom they exchange mutual support and cooperation.

Teton Lakota activist Leonard Peltier is taken to a waiting helicopter from his Canadian prison cell for deportation back to the United States in December 1976. Peltier was accused and later convicted of murdering two FBI agents on the Pine Ridge reservation, but his case is regarded by many as a severe miscarriage of justice.

Today, the Teton use education as a means of preserving their language, history, and cultural heritage, as well as a way to prepare a new generation of leaders to face the challenge of the future.

After gifts are given, speeches are offered by men who are specially selected by the host. Speeches include moral lessons directed at young people, teaching them traditional values of harmony and helpfulness to others. The men's speeches are punctuated and followed by a chorus of approval from women in attendance. Afterwards, a traditional feast is shared by all.

Other aspects of Teton ceremonial life continue to be important to many in the various reservation communities. Followers of traditional Teton religion mark many of the ancient Sacred Rites performed by their ancestors. Sun

Dances are held often, especially in rural communities where traditions remain strongest. In addition, many people seek to obtain support and instruction from spirits through individual Vision Quests. And many people seek advice and care given by traditional healers when they suffer from illness or other misfortunes.

Another aspect of life that is critical to maintaining Teton traditions is knowledge and use of the Lakota language. The language is spoken by many Teton on the reservations. People living in rural areas and those involved in traditional lifeways are more likely to speak Lakota fluently. Lakota is used especially in traditional religious and social contexts.

In order to ensure continuation of Lakota, the language is taught to children in schools on the reservations. It is taught at all levels of education, including elementary and high school, as well as at the two Teton community colleges, one on Pine Ridge and the other on the Rosebud Reservation.

Schools serving Teton children and adults also offer courses in Indian studies programs that are dedicated to preserving Teton history and culture.

The Teton continue to balance the changes brought about by their circumstances with the valued traditions of their heritage. Problems of finding employment on or near reservations still affect hopes for their prosperity. Economic enterprises have been established by the tribe and by individuals, but they are often in danger of failure because of lack of capital to invest and expand. Although many people do find jobs nearby, rates of unemployment and underemployment remain high.

Still, the reservation communities survive and provide social support and nurturance for their members. Popula-tions on the reservations continue to grow. According to census statistics for 1990, the Pine Ridge Reservation is the largest, with 10,455 Teton residents. Rosebud is next, with 6,883 members. Somewhat smaller in number is the Cheyenne River Reservation; it has 5,100 residents. The smallest reservation is Standing Rock, with a population of 2,034.

There are many other Teton people living in communities away from the reservations. Some live in nearby towns and cities in South Dakota, North Dakota, and Nebraska. Others live in distant places throughout the United States. Many of these people, though, maintain strong ties to their home reservations, returning as often as possible to visit and participate in family and community events.

Bonds among the Teton remain strong. Although divided by territory, and sometimes by attitudes and politics, they remain convinced that they must work together in order to achieve common goals and to provide a setting of harmony and prosperity for themselves and their descendants. Such was the wish of the Teton centuries ago, and such is the hope of the Teton today. ▲

BIBLIOGRAPHY

Deloria, Vine, Jr. *Behind the Trail of Broken Treaties*. New York: Dell, 1974.

———. *Custer Died for Your Sins*. New York: Avon Books, 1969.

Grobsmith, Elizabeth. *Lakota of the Rosebud: A Contemporary Ethnography*. New York: Holt, Rinehart & Winston, 1981.

Josephy, Alvin, Jr. "Crazy Horse." In *The Patriot Chiefs: A Chronicle of American Indian Resistance*. New York: Viking Books, 1958.

Kehoe, Alice. *The Ghost Dance: Ethnohistory and Revitalization*. New York: Holt, Rinehart & Winston, 1989.

Mooney, James. *The Ghost Dance Religion and the Sioux Outbreak of 1890*. Chicago: University of Chicago Press, 1965.

Neihardt, John. *Black Elk Speaks: Being the Life Story of a Holy Man of the Oglala Sioux*. Lincoln: University of Nebraska Press, 1961.

Powers, William. *Oglala Religion*. Norman: University of Oklahoma Press, 1985.

Price, John. *Native Studies: American and Canadian Indians*. Toronto: McGraw-Hill/Ryerson, 1978.

Spencer, Robert, et al. *Native Americans*. New York: Macmillan, 1981.

Sword et al. "Wakan." In *Teachings from the American Earth: Indian Religion & Philosophy*. Edited by Dennis Tedlock and Barbara Tedlock. New York: Liveright, 1988.

Talbot, Steve. *Roots of Oppression*. New York: International, 1981.

THE TETON SIOUX AT A GLANCE

TRIBE *Teton Lakota*
CULTURE AREA *Northern plains of the United States*
GEOGRAPHY *Minnesota, North and South Dakota, Nebraska, and Wyoming*
LINGUISTIC FAMILY *Siouan*
CURRENT POPULATION *Approximately 25,000 on reservations in South Dakota*
STATUS *Tribal reservations in South Dakota: Cheyenne River, Lower Brulé, Pine Ridge, Rosebud, Standing Rock*

GLOSSARY

agent A person appointed by the Bureau of Indian Affairs to supervise U.S. government programs on a reservation and/or in a specific region.

American Indian Movement (AIM) Native rights organization, founded in 1968, that used militant tactics to draw attention to the adverse conditions facing Native Americans.

annuity Money or goods paid yearly or at a regular interval.

band A loosely organized group of people who are bound together by the need for food and defense, by family ties, and/or by other common interests.

bilateral descent Kinship traced through both the mother's and the father's family.

breechcloth A strip of animal skin or cloth that is drawn between the legs and hung from a belt tied around the waist.

Bureau of Indian Affairs A federal government agency now within the Department of the Interior. Originally intended to manage trade and other relations with Indians, the BIA now seeks to develop and implement programs that encourage Indians to manage their own affairs and to improve their educational opportunities and general social and economic well-being.

counting coup System of ranking acts of bravery in war, with the highest honor going to the warrior who attacked an enemy at close contact.

culture The learned behavior of humans; nonbiological, socially taught activities; the way of life of a group of people.

Dawes Act The 1887 federal law, also known as the General Allotment Act, that called for dividing reservation land into small allotments assigned to individual families. This policy undermined the traditional native way of life.

dialect A regional variant of a particular language with unique elements of grammar, pronunciation, and vocabulary.

Ghost Dance religion A religion begun in 1889 that prophesied the end of the world, followed by a return to traditional Native American life. Believers participated in ceremonies and dances of hope and celebration, which were eventually banned by the U.S. government.

Heyoka A prestigious Teton social group whose members were called by spirit visions and had to do everything in reverse.

Indian Reorganization Act (IRA) The 1934 federal law that ended the policy of allotting plots of land to individuals and encouraged the development of reservation communities. The act also provided for the creation of autonomous tribal governments.

nomadic Moving from place to place, often depending on the season or food supply, and establishing only temporary camps.

peace chief An older man who was respected for his intelligence, compassion, and skill in hunting and healing.

reservation A tract of land retained by Indians for their own occupation and use.

roach A young man's hairstyle in which the sides of the head are shaved, with only the hair in the center allowed to grow.

Sun Dance A sacred ritual performed every summer in which the Teton give thanks for good fortune by performing different acts. In the most dramatic facet of the ritual, men pierce their flesh and dance around a pole until they are torn free.

sweat bath A ritual purification, considered sacred by the Teton, that prepares people to face the world of supernatural beings.

tipi An easily transportable, cone-shaped home, rounded at the base and tapered to an open smoke hole at the top, that is made of buffalo hides and wooden poles.

treaty A contract negotiated between sovereign nations. Treaties between the U.S. government and the Indian tribes dealt with the cessation of military action, the surrender of political independence, the establishment of boundaries, terms of land sales, and related matters.

tribe A society consisting of several or many separate communities united by kinship, culture, language, and other social institutions, including clans, religious organizations, and warrior societies.

Vision Quest A sacred ritual in which a person, spiritually purified through a fast and a sweat bath, went off alone for four days of fasting and praying in order to receive visions from a supernatural spirit who would act as a personal guardian.

war chief A younger man who, while brave and daring in leading men in warfare, was under the authority of the older peace chiefs.

INDEX

PICTURE CREDITS

NANCY BONVILLAIN is an adjunct professor at the New School for Social Research. She has a Ph.D. in anthropology from Columbia University. Dr. Bonvillain has written a grammar book and dictionary of the Mohawk language as well as *The Huron* (1989), *The Mohawk* (1992), *The Hopi* (1994), and *Black Hawk* (1994) for Chelsea House.

FRANK W. PORTER III, general editor of INDIANS OF NORTH AMERICA, is director of the Chelsea House Foundation for American Indian Studies. He holds a B.A., M.A., and Ph.D. from the University of Maryland. He has done extensive research concerning the Indians of Maryland and Delaware and is the author of numerous articles on their history, archaeology, geography, and ethnography. He was formerly director of the Maryland Commission on Indian Affairs and American Indian Research and Resource Institute, Gettysburg, Pennsylvania, and he has received grants from the Delaware Humanities Forum, the Maryland Committee for the Humanities, the Ford Foundation, and the National Endowment for the Humanities, among others. Dr. Porter is the author of *The Bureau of Indian Affairs* in the Chelsea House KNOW YOUR GOVERNMENT series.